A structured approach to
Pascal

The Irwin Series in Information and Decision Sciences

Consulting Editors   Robert B. Fetter   Claude McMillan
                                   Yale University   University of Colorado

A structured approach to

Pascal

BILLY K. WALKER
Department of Engineering
University of Oklahoma

1983
RICHARD D. IRWIN, INC.
Homewood, Illinois   60430

ISBN 0-256-02827-3

Library of Congress Catalog Card No. 82–81948

Printed in the United States of America

1 2 3 4 5 6 7 8 9 0 ML 0 9 8 7 6 5 4 3

DEDICATION

There are so many people to whom I would like to dedicate this book that it is hard to know where to start.

Foremost among my friends and relatives, is my lovely and supportive wife, Anita, who has stood by me in times both good and bad. Without her, I could not possibly have managed this or any other project of such magnitude.

I must also mention my wonderful parents, Jack and Jo, who raised me in both an academic atmosphere and a warm and loving home, and without whose example I wouldn't have found the profession which I love so much.

A long time ago a friend suggested that I should write a book, and I told that friend that if I ever did, I would dedicate it to him. Therefore, this book is also dedicated to Melvin R. Kerchee, Senior, and the Comanche War Society, who were among the first to say "Why don't you write a book?"

Finally I must dedicate this text to the reader, who I sincerely hope will enjoy it!

Preface

A *Structured Approach to Pascal* is intended for computer beginners, not computer experts. Upon completion of this text, readers should be able to write useful programs in the Pascal language, and they should be fully prepared to continue their studies using any of the more advanced texts on the market.

Perhaps *A Structured Approach to Pascal* will also prove useful to those individuals who already possess a modest knowledge of some other programming language. Any dialect of BASIC, FORTRAN, COBOL, or virtually any other language could serve as a basis for use of this book, though one would not have to be an expert with any language.

A Structured Approach to Pascal should be suitable for

1. Computer beginners or persons in independent study situations.
2. Use as a supplementary text in an advanced course.
3. Use as a complete text for an introductory course.
4. Use as a text in a course including several programming languages.

A Structured Approach to Pascal is intended as a "friend" to help you on your way in the study of Pascal. No matter how you use this book, one of its most valuable features is its collection of exercises. The problems have been selected to illustrate various properties of Pascal as well as for their own (we hope!) intrinsic interest. The problem sets in Chapter 10 are marked according to their difficulty, and alternative problems are provided for students of the engineering sciences and for students with an interest in business or managerial sciences. Some of the engineering exercises are quite mathematical in nature, while the problems for the business sciences require very little mathematics. The problems which require mathematics are marked as being nonessential to the study of this book.

It is quite impossible to learn Pascal (or any other language, whether for computers or people) without practice—in this case, writing programs. Consequently, the reader is admonished to strive to complete as many of the problems and exercises as time and ambition will permit. The working programs presented in Appendix B provide a wealth of examples that may prove very useful. The student is encouraged to "mine" this trove freely.

Good Luck as you study Pascal—above all, ***have fun!***

Acknowledgments

The author gratefully acknowledges Springer-Verlag publishing company for permission to use some of the material in Appendix A. This material originally appeared in the *Pascal User Manual and Report,* by Kathleen Jensen and Niklaus Wirth (2d ed.).

The following reviewers of the text deserve thanks for their suggestions and constructive criticisms: William Carlborg, Prairie State College; Don R. Cartlidge, New Mexico State University; William C. Covey, III, The Florida State University; John Lushbaugh, University of South Dakota; Kevin L. Shannon, Orange Coast College; and Hoyt D. Warner, The Hartford Graduate Center.

The author is also grateful to Chris Barnett for typing some of the material in Chapters 4 and 5, and to my favorite proofreaders, my wife Anita and my parents Jack and Jo.

Finally, the long-suffering computer science students at the University of Oklahoma deserve special mention for the many helpful suggestions and honest criticisms which they (sometimes gleefully) offered as this book was being prepared.

Billy K. Walker

Contents

1.0

Introduction

1.1   A DISCUSSION OF THE NAME *Pascal*

There are many computer languages in use today—perhaps several thousand! Some of the more common are BASIC, FORTRAN, COBOL, and Pascal. Of these four names, three are acronyms. FORTRAN stands for *FOR*mula *TRAN*slation; BASIC for *B*eginner's *A*ll-purpose *S*ymbolic *In*struction *C*ode; and COBOL for *CO*mmon *B*usiness *O*riented *L*anguage. Since these are acronyms, it is proper to capitalize all of the letters in the words; hence FORTRAN, not Fortran or fortran.

Pascal, however, is a man's name. The inventors of the Pascal language named it after French mathematician Blaise Pascal, who lived from 1623 to 1662 and who is responsible for, among other things, the famous Pascal's triangle of algebra. Since Pascal is a proper name and not an acronym, it should have only its first letter capitalized. In fact, PASCAL is somewhat improper, except in certain contexts, where all letters of surrounding words happen to be capitalized as well.

Throughout this book we will blatantly abuse the usage of this word, usually without apology. This abuse will be necessitated in part by the fact that we will write all computer listings using capital letters and occasionally will use capital letters in other contexts as a means of emphasis. Of course, both the reader and the author really know better.

1.2   THE GO TO STATEMENT

If you have ever programmed a computer before, you have probably used the GO TO statement. If you have never programmed a computer, you may skip this section!

The GO TO statement is intended to cause a program to branch to a different location in its sequence. In many languages, branching is neces-

1

sary in order for programs to carry out such logical operations as IF . . . GO TO. . . .

The use of the GO TO can make a program very hard to read, however, because it often obscures the flow of logic. One of the objectives of structured programming is to make programs easy to read, even for the person who did not write the original code. As an example, consider the following short program:

```
10 read (limit)
20 if limit < = 27 then go to 50
30 if limit > 27 then go to 80
40 limit = limit + 1
50 limit = limit − 1
60 go to 100
80 print limit
100 end
```

What does the program do? If you were presented with this program and asked to interpret it, you could do so, after some thought. But what if the program had 1,000 lines of code instead of 9? The use of the GO TO can cause a lot of grief.

One goal of modern programming thought is to make programs as readable as possible. Pascal has been designed with this goal in mind. One of the most startling things about Pascal to the novice user is the absence of the need for the GO TO statement. (There are exceptions, of course.)

Careful construction of the syntax of Pascal allows the proper transfer of control from one portion of a program to another in most instances without the necessity for the GO TO statement. (In fact, in many Pascal implementations, it is possible to "turn off" the GO TO altogether, making use of the GO TO a syntax error!) This, perhaps more than any other single feature, makes Pascal an eminently readable language.

1.3   TOP-DOWN STRUCTURED DESIGN

Two concepts about programming—*top-down* and *structured design*— have been highly touted in recent publications, and quite a bit of confusion has arisen about the terms. In this section we explore some of their meanings and implications.

Suppose that you (perhaps through some indiscretion) have been given the assignment of making small rocks out of big rocks. (Freshmen may consider this predicament not unlike their own.) In fact, suppose that you really messed up, and as a result you have been asked to reduce Pike's Peak to gravel. There might be several approaches to this problem. If you start at the base of the mountain and work your way through it, you risk having the mountain collapse on you. On a more philosophical level, it is

Proper top down design can keep the roof from caving in

sometimes hard to tell just where the mountain starts in the first place so that you know where to begin working.

Clearly, to "gravelize" a mountain one must start at some easily defined place that presents no danger from falling rocks. In other words, start at the top of the mountain, not the bottom, and proceed to wield the hammer.

Suppose now that someone really wants to get even with you (perhaps you were caught plagiarizing a program!) and you are asked to reduce Pike's Peak, not to gravel, but to sand instead. Perhaps the easiest way to solve this new problem is to solve two problems: first, reduce the mountain to gravel and then pound the gravel to sand. This process represents a *refinement* of a problem. Let's examine it more closely.

Consider Figure 1–1. Here we have used a box to represent a task (in this case, making gravel).

If we are required to make sand instead of gravel, we use two separate processes, one after the other. Deciding on these steps is a way of making a *structured design,* albeit a simple one in this case. Essential to this pro-

Figure 1–1

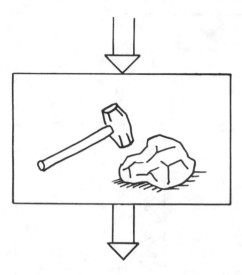

cedure is the knowledge of what goes into each process and what comes out of each process (see Figure 1–2).

Let's construct a different hypothetical example. In the following account, the names of the entities involved have been changed, and liberties taken with some of the historical perspective.

Just a few years ago there existed a giant software company which was in the business of writing programs for other companies to use. This company was known as the BII (Biggest In Industry) Company.

The BII Company was approached by the Goodblimp Corporation and asked to write a program that would keep track of the incredibly diverse Goodblimp inventory (it takes lots of parts to make a blimp). After suitable corporate meetings it was agreed that BII would provide the program—for $1 million and in five years. At the time, Goodblimp considered it an exceedingly attractive deal and quickly signed the contract.

BII, with the ink still wet on the contract, rushed out into the world and hired a young whiz kid to write the program, promising him an exorbitant salary and a five-year contract.

The Whiz, as he was known, proved worth his keep. After three years and two months, he had the program three-fourths completed. He still lacked several key parts, and he had not yet documented any of his program, but it was clear that all deadlines were going to be met and the contract would be fulfilled.

BII heaped blessings on the Whiz, to be sure to keep him happy until delivery was made. Alas, the Whiz had an unfortunate encounter with an enraged mountain goat while in the midst of laboring in his private rock garden. The encounter left the goat with a mild headache and a bad temper, but it left the world without the Whiz.

Figure 1–2

MOUNTAIN
IN

GRAVEL
OUT

GRAVEL
IN

SAND
OUT

When it came time for BII to try to salvage the remains of the programming project, it was apparent that the project had departed the earth with the Whiz, since the key parts were locked in his head, and documentation was dreadful if it existed at all.

In short, BII got taken to the cleaners in the courts for defaulting on the Goodblimp contract, and Goodblimp went looking elsewhere for computer programs.

Out of the wreckage blossomed an idea. "Suppose we hired lots of programmers and had each person work on only one part of a program," offered one executive. "Then, when all the parts were finished, we could just stack all the card decks together and run the whole thing."

Of course, it really wasn't that easy, since a lot of protocol was involved, and many technical decisions had to be made regarding just *how* one might break a large program into smaller portions—but in essence the idea worked. Collecting together a set of rules for programmers to follow enabled them to apply a team effort to the writing of computer programs. Some of these rules were technical in nature, and others were simply agreements on how best to do things.

The point is that a *discipline* was imposed on programmers. This discipline involved, not only technical rules, but also rules about documentation and testing of programming parts, and a set of protocols designed to allow the stacking of various parts of a program into a workable finished product.

The BII Company tried this approach. It hired several young programmers, paid them good salaries, and hired a supervisor to oversee the work. Then BII executives went to see Goodblimp.

At Goodblimp, the BII Company offered to write an inventory-control program and deliver it in six months. The price tag was quoted at $12 million! Goodblimp, in spite of its previous experience, was by now in desperate need of the program. They also considered that the program would save them $25 million over five years if they had it; so they were not discouraged by the high cost.

In short, BII delivered the goods, even though one of the junior programmers was caught in an updraft while skydiving. He had followed the protocol, and another programmer was able to pick up where the first one had left off, largely because of the documentation that had been left behind. Goodblimp was happy, BII was ecstatic, and even the lost skydiver finally came to roost in a pine tree in New Mexico; so the whole concept became firmly entrenched at BII, where it served in good stead through other lucrative contracts.

While this account is of course fictionalized, it contains some elements of truth. Good planning and careful documentation allow programming efforts that would simply be impossible otherwise. The loose "bag of rules" that govern such projects has been called *structured programming*. There is some argument over just what rules should be in the "bag," and different companies have different ideas, but the concept remains the same. The objective is to impose a discipline on the art of programming so that workable programs that are easily documented and even easy to read can be created routinely, with relative ease, and in timely fashion.

Many concepts are embodied in the notion of structured programming. One very important concept requires that programs be written in modules. Each module should have a single, specific, easily tested function and be constructed in such a way that it can easily interact with other modules. In essence one should be able to "stack the card decks" and expect them to work.

As one would expect, there are many rules which appear in published form and purport to allow one to write "modularized" programs. Instead of reciting some particular set of these rules (there are many versions), we prefer to abstract the essence of the lessons learned in the two situations presented above. This essence is easily stated:

1. Start by stating an objective and specifying a process to accomplish this objective.

2. Break the process into a series of steps which follow one after the other.

3. Break each of these steps into successively smaller steps, until it becomes clear how to accomplish each step.

4. Accomplish each step.

5. Use the completed steps as "building blocks" to construct the program itself.

Item 5 presents some problems of its own. The programmer must not only break the program into steps but also be sure to use steps that can be used as building blocks. This requirement leads us temporarily astray. We will return to these five points after we divert for a few minutes to a discussion of building blocks.

1.4 BUILDING BLOCKS

Suppose that one is given a part of a program, represented by the box in Figure 1–3.

Figure 1–3

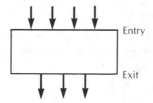

This program part has several entry points and several exit points. That is, there are several pathways that take us into the program part; and, depending on actions in the box, we can leave it by any of several routes. If we attempt to stack a second box underneath the first one, we would have to be very careful that the second box provided an appropriate number of entry points so that the two boxes would properly match. This is illustrated in Figure 1–4.

Figure 1–4

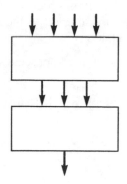

Random building blocks

If we insist on writing boxes (program parts or program modules) with multiple entry points and multiple exit points, we must carefully keep track of just which boxes will stack on top of which other boxes. That is, we must be sure that a box with three exit lines rests on top of a box with three entry points, and so on.

A more sensible approach is to standardize the number of entry points and exit points that program modules may have, requiring that all modules conform to this standard and are thus essentially "stackable". We still have to write correct modules that work as we had hoped, and we still have to stack them in the proper order, but with agreement on the number of entry points and exit points, we will whip a large part of the problem. A little thought will convince the reader that the only really reasonable standard number for entry and exit points is *one*.

We are imposing a discipline on ourselves by requiring that every module of a program must have only a single entry point and a single exit point. This requirement at least ensures that the output of one module can easily be directed to form the input for another module. A glance at Figure 1−5 makes it clear that the program modules on the left are stackable and those on the right are not.

Perhaps the most important single tenet of structured programming, then, is this: program modules must have only a single entry and a single exit.

Now, as promised, we return to the five steps we outlined earlier. Pascal (along with some other languages) is designed to provide us with build-

Figure 1–5

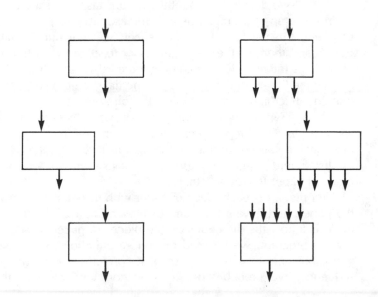

ing blocks which have single entry and single exit points (this is not true of FORTRAN or BASIC). In Chapter 4 we will discover that most of Pascal's program constructions are already provided with a single entry point and a single exit point. This is one of the major reasons that Pascal is known as a highly structured language. It is actually difficult (though by no means impossible) to write an unstructured program in Pascal!

In the next section we will write a program that illustrates the concepts of top-down programming and structured programming. Since these concepts are not really dependent on language, we will choose as our programming language the English language.

1.5   WRITING (IN ENGLISH) A SAMPLE STRUCTURED PROGRAM

As our assignment, we will assume that we are to present a book report to a class. Our first attempt at a program to accomplish this assignment might appear as follows:

FIND THE BOOK
READ THE BOOK
PREPARE THE REPORT
PRESENT THE ORAL REPORT
GET RID OF THE BOOK

We realize fairly quickly that these steps outline the big jobs that have to be accomplished but that a lot of detail is missing. We might make a second attempt by refining the steps somewhat. If we were describing the process to a computer, we would be careful to make each step much more specific. If we decide to continue with our task, we should tackle the program one step at a time. It is not unreasonable to prepare several pieces of paper. On the top of the first sheet, we will put the label "Find the Book" and then list the steps necessary to accomplish that task. Some of these steps might include searching the card catalog in the library, or even finding the library in the first place. The list should be detailed enough that one could actually acquire a book by following it.

Now we will label a second piece of paper "Reading the Book." On it we will write the steps necessary to reading the book, perhaps including even such details as turning on the light if necessary. If a particular task on the list should require an explanation of its own, we will prepare another piece of paper that details that task.

After preparing each piece of paper with its detailed steps, we can stack the papers and have a program for presenting a book report. All we have to do is follow the directions on the pieces of paper. When we were writing the program, we devoted our entire attention, not to the whole program, but only to whatever part of it concerned us at the moment. Consequently, we probably did a better job with each of the parts, and

The first brick

eventually with the whole program, than we would have done if we had been required to write the entire program in one pass on a single sheet of paper.

The moral is simple: divide the large task into many smaller ones. Whip the smaller problems, and then you have quite naturally completed the larger task by simply accomplishing the little ones! Divide and conquer!

2.0

The general form of a Pascal program

2.1   GETTING STARTED

In this chapter we will explore the various activities necessary to writing a Pascal program which can then be run on a computer.

Computers are actually exceedingly *dumb* machines. They not only must have every step of a procedure described to them, but they must also have the steps described to them in a certain way. We use a computer language to describe the steps of a particular problem to the machine. There are many such languages, one of which is known as Pascal.

We have two fundamental tasks confronting us. We must decide how to solve a particular problem, and then we must provide a computer with a set of directions (called a *program*) which tells the computer how to solve the problem. The first task, that of deciding how to solve a particular problem (either with or without a computer), is known as determining the *logic* of the problem. The second task, that of communicating this logic to the machine, is called *programming*.

The computer, idiot that it is, must have every single step of the logic carefully spelled out to it. Furthermore, the steps must be described to the machine in a certain fashion. If the steps are presented according to a certain set of rules, then the machine is capable of translating the instructions into something meaningful to itself.

If we want to tell the computer to add two numbers together, the computer must first determine what electronic operations to perform to accomplish an ADD.

Since the computer is not really very smart, it expects its instructions to be presented according to a set of rules that enable it to ascertain the exact meaning of each instruction.

As a consequence, programmers are faced with following these rules when they write programs. The Pascal language consists of a collection of

Getting started

"rules" which allows a computer to understand the electronic meaning of the instructions that the programmer gives to the machine. This chapter provides an overview of these rules.

A Pascal program consists of several parts. These parts must be presented to the machine in a certain order, since each depends somewhat upon the ones preceding. Each part is made up of subparts, which communicate directions to the machine.

Figure 2–1
Two Pascal programs

```
PROGRAM NOTHING;
  BEGIN
  (* DO NOTHING *)
  END.
```
A Pascal program to do
absolutely nothing

```
PROGRAM HOWDY (OUTPUT);
  BEGIN
    WRITELN ('HELLO')
  END.
```
A Pascal program to write
"HELLO" on the screen

The main divisions, or parts, of a Pascal program are presented in the next section. Since every Pascal program must follow this general outline, it is probably worth your while to commit it to memory. Actually, this won't take much effort, since after you write a couple of programs the sequence will become second nature anyway.

Just to give you something to look at, Figure 2–1 shows two complete Pascal programs that perform trivial tasks. You can probably understand them, even without having studied Pascal at all!

2.1.1   The program outline

Please refer to Figure 2–2 throughout the rest of this section.

Figure 2–2 delineates the proper order of various portions of a Pascal program. This order must be followed in any Pascal program (including those of Figure 2–1, which perform only trivial tasks). However, some parts of the program outline may not be necessary. For instance, if you never use GO TO statements, you will not need the Label Declarations portion of the outline; so it can simply be left out. The program outline is sufficiently important that it should be committed to memory. Each part of the program outline may depend on other parts that appear above it. For instance, a type declaration may depend on a constant definition made earlier in the program. This is the main reason for demanding that the program outline be followed exactly.

Figure 2–2
Outline of a Pascal program

```
PROGRAM HEADING
LABEL DECLARATIONS
CONSTANT DEFINITIONS
TYPE DECLARATIONS
VARIABLE DECLARATIONS
PROCEDURE AND FUNCTION DEFINITIONS
MAIN BODY OF PROGRAM
```

We will eventually discuss each part of the program outline. Before you finish the book, you will have the ability to write a Pascal program that uses all the parts of the program outline, but in the beginning we will be writing much simpler programs.

In this section we will discuss several diverse topics which, when integrated, will allow us to write Pascal programs. Of necessity, when we first present these topics, they will seem unrelated, but each of them is necessary to the writing of Pascal programs. In this preliminary section, we will emphasize the concepts of *program heading, constants, type,* and *variables,* and mention only briefly the other portions.

Heading
Labels
Constants
Types
Variables
Procedures and functions
Main body

2.1.2 Program heading

The first line of a Pascal program is the *program heading*. This line tells the machine the name of the program and also whether the program will expect input, produce output, or both.

A simple form of the program heading is

PROGRAM PROGRAMNAME (INPUT,OUTPUT);

where PROGRAMNAME is any name that you desire. (It must begin with a letter.)

If the program expects input from the keyboard at some point, then INPUT must be present. If the program will produce output (most do!), then OUTPUT must be present as well. Later modification of this line will enable the program to input from, or output to, disk files.

Occasionally (as in Figure 2–1) there are no input data, since some programs do not require input. In that case, the program header appears as

PROGRAM PROGRAMNAME (OUTPUT);

The parentheses are important, as is the semicolon!

2.1.3 Label declarations

This is one of the portions we can leave out for now. In the Label Declarations section we identify to the machine those points to which control will pass from a GO TO statement. Since GO TO statements are discouraged in this book, and since the Label Declaration section is not present unless GO TO statements are used, we will skip this section for now.

If you ever do have a real need for labels, they must be identified in the label section, which must appear in its proper place in the program out-line. But chances are that you will rarely, if ever, need label declarations.

2.1.4   Constant definitions

A *constant* is something that does not change. Consequently, if there is some entity in a computer program that remains unchanged throughout the running of the program, you might appropriately declare it as a con-stant. An example might be the value of pi (π).

If we write a computer program that computes the area or circumfer-ence of a circle many times, no matter how many times we run that pro-gram, the value of pi never changes. Consequently, we might profit by establishing a symbol, say PI, for the value of pi, and using it instead of 3.14159. . . .

Pascal allows the substitution of symbols for quantities that never change. Such a substitution should be established in the Constant Defini-tions section of a Pascal program (see the program outline). Incidentally, proper use of constants can increase the running efficiency of your pro-gram considerably in some implementations.

Remember, a constant is something that does not change its value. That something can be numerical, such as the value of pi, or it can be a char-acter, such as the letter A. We will find ways of taking advantage of con-stants in later programs. For now, just be sure that the concept of a con-stant is reasonable to you.

As an example, we could use the following code as part of a Pascal program:

```
CONST PI = 3.14159;
```

Now, anywhere in the program that we need to use the value 3.14159, we can just write the symbol PI instead. Of course, we may also have declared other constants, such as E (2.71828).

2.1.5   Type declarations

The concept of *type* seems to bother many beginners in Pascal program-ming. Fundamental to the concept of type is the fact that the computer stores different entities in different ways. For instance, the letter A is stored differently than the number 1.0. Both of these are stored differently than the whole number 2. When a computer is storing numbers, it needs to have knowledge of the presence or absence of a decimal point in order to select the right storage category.

Whole numbers, which are numbers that do not contain decimal points, are called *integers* and are stored in a certain fashion by the machine. Numbers which do contain decimal points, such as 26.7, are called *real numbers* and are stored in a different fashion. Letters are said to be *characters,* and they are stored yet differently. There is still another type, called *boolean,* which we will study later.

Using these fundamental types—real, integer, char, and boolean—it is possible to make more complicated types of entities. We might make up a word by using several characters strung together. If we wish to do so, we are at liberty to create our own types at will in the type declaration portion of the program.

The important thing to remember at this stage is that (almost without exception) *every single symbol in a Pascal program has a type.*

The fundamental types that we are concerned with at the moment are:

REAL—numbers which contain decimal points.

INTEGER—numbers which do not contain decimal points (whole numbers).

CHAR—symbols which represent letters of the alphabet.

2.1.6   Variable declarations

Since we have defined constants as things that cannot change, it makes sense to define variables as entities that can change within the body of a program. For instance, if we instruct a computer to read a name from a list and then write out the name it read, and we run the program many times, we will find that the name can change every time we run the program. The symbols that we use to stand for things which can vary or change within a program are called *variables.*

The computer handles constants and variables somewhat differently and consequently needs to know what symbols we are using for each. We inform the computer of the symbolism that we choose to use for variables in the Variable Declarations section of the program.

In our example of computing the areas and circumferences of various circles, for instance, we see that the value of the radius of a circle may change every time we run the program. Thus it might be appropriate to declare RADIUS as a variable. Since the area also takes on different values corresponding to different radii, we should declare AREA as a variable as well. We could then compute the area of a circle by

AREA := PI * RADIUS * RADIUS

where PI is the constant that we defined in the Constant Definitions section above. For the moment, we will rely on your instinct to allow you to read this sentence as "Let AREA equal PI times RADIUS times RADIUS." Section 2.2.1 will be devoted to removing some of the mystery of the symbolism.

Remember, constants never change value, while variables can and usually do change value. When we tell the computer that we are using a variable, we must also tell the computer what the type of that variable is, so that the computer can reserve the proper amount of storage for it.

2.1.7   Procedure and Function definitions

Procedures and functions will soon become a major part of most of our Pascal programs, but we will not discuss them at length until a later chapter. For the present, we can leave this portion out of our programs, since the program we are about to write contains no procedures or functions. However, you should be aware of their proper place in the program outline, and that is the reason we have mentioned them here.

For those who have programmed before, procedures and functions are the subprograms of Pascal, similar to the subroutines of other languages.

In summary.   Remember that *every symbol that appears in a Pascal program has a type.*[1] Pascal requires that we tell the computer which symbols stand for entities of which type. We give the machine this information in the Variables Declarations portion of the program, as well as in the Constant Definitions section and the Label Declarations section. It is this requirement that gives Pascal one of its most important strengths, and conversely, it is this very point that provides much of the frustration for the neophyte programmer.

Type is discussed at greater length in Chapter 6.

In the Variable Declarations section, we specifically mention every symbol which can change its value in the program, and we inform the machine of its type, so that proper storage can be allocated for the variable. Remember that *type* can be any of the predefined types, such as REAL or INTEGER, or it can be defined to fit the programmer's needs.

The most important point here is that every variable in the program must be mentioned specifically in the Variable Declarations section. This means that the programmer will have to plan the program before it is written!

2.1.8   Main body of the program

The main body of the program consists of a single *compound statement,* made up of many statements contained between an initial BEGIN and a final END. The final END of the program is followed by a period, not a semicolon.

In order to illustrate all of the foregoing discussion, we will write a short and complete Pascal program in the following sections. The reader is invited to load it up and try it.

We have spent a great deal of time so far trying to provide a broad view of the various parts of a Pascal program. As with any language, a myriad

---

[1]An expert on Pascal might take minor exception to this statement. However, few would quarrel with the philosophy which inspired it, and as a rule of thumb, it must stand.

of details enter into writing a Pascal program. (Witness the many details of punctuation and sentence construction that must be observed in order to write a paragraph in the English language!) As programming languages go, Pascal has comparatively few noxious details, and most of the details are actually helpful in writing programs, once you get the hang of them.

In the next section we will explore a few of the more important details so that we will be able to read and understand an example Pascal program without undue hardship.

2.2   SOME ODDS AND ENDS WE NEED TO KNOW

Our goal for this chapter is to write a complete and "runnable" Pascal program. However, there are several loose ends which must be tied up before we proceed. The next several pages are devoted to such loose ends and should not be skipped.

We will write a short and complete Pascal program that will serve as an illustration of some of the concepts that we have discussed. The example is somewhat contrived, since we are attempting to illuminate several points. If we only desired to accomplish a particular task, we could probably do so in an easier fashion.

The first "odd and end" that should be mentioned is the *comment*. Comments are just that—remarks placed in a program by the person who wrote it to provide annotations about parts of the program. In Pascal, comments are written like this:

(* anything you want goes here *).

By the way, in Pascal we can place comments almost anywhere. (Just don't break a word in two.)

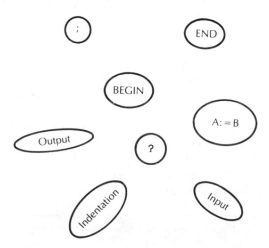

Properly and lavishly commented programs are a joy to read and are *always* easier for a programmer to deal with. Don't be afraid to use lots of comments. Later, you will gain some experience as to just what should be commented and what should not, but for the moment, it is safe to err on the side of providing superfluous comments rather than not enough.

2.2.1   The assignment statement and arithmetic operators

In Pascal, the assignment operator is := and not the = of many languages. (Type a colon followed by an equals sign without a space in between.)

Legal assignments can be made only between notations of the same type.[2] For example, let us suppose that we have declared A and B to be variables of type INTEGER, X and Y to be variables of type REAL, and LETTER and STUFF to be variables of type CHAR. Then the following assignments are legal (note the semicolons!):

```
A := 1;            A := 1 + A;
B := 7;            A := A + B;
A := B;            B := -104;
X := 8.2;          Y := -9.0;
X := Y;            X := Y - 10.0;
X := X + Y;        LETTER := 'W';
STUFF := 'J';      LETTER := STUFF;
```

The following are not legal assignments:

```
A := X; (* A is INTEGER, while X is REAL *)
LETTER := A; (* LETTER is CHAR, while A is INTEGER *)
A := STUFF; (* A is INTEGER, while STUFF is CHAR *)
LETTER := STUFF + 1; (* lots wrong here—you can't perform arith-
      metic with letters *)
LETTER := LETTER + STUFF; (* same reasoning *)
A := B + 7; (* is anything wrong? *)
```

In later chapters we will discover a method to learn when the semicolon is required and when it is merely optional; we will also study semicolons in Appendix A, where we deal with syntax diagrams. For the time being, use a semicolon after assignment statements, and you will be right almost all the time.

When you read the above discussion, you probably were willing to assume that + meant "add" and that − meant "subtract." You may even have noticed two usages of the − symbol. The assignment statements

```
A := X - Y;
```

---

[2]Now that we have stated such an easy-to-remember rule, we must mention the exception. Many compilers allow the assignment X := Y where the left-hand symbol is of type REAL and the right-hand symbol is of type INTEGER.

and

A := −27;

represent two different usages of the − symbol. The first usage means "subtract," while the second means "negate." Pascal is able to tell from the context which of these two meanings is to be used.

Other possible operations are:

A := B * C;

which means "let A have the value of B multiplied by C."

A := B / C;

which means "let A have the value of B divided by C."

Actually, there is considerably more to division than this. It makes sense that division by zero will result in an error; so the programmer must take some pains to avoid it. Also, a more subtle problem can arise.

We may decide to divide B by C to derive A. However, it does not necessarily follow that A is of the same type as B and C. For instance, suppose B and C are both of type INTEGER, say with B := 2 and C := 3. But if we write A := B/C we may discover that A is not of the same type as B and C. Remember, A had to be declared to be of a certain type long before we ever used it. If we had decided that A was to be of type REAL, then the division would proceed without incident, and A would attain the value of .66666 . . . to however many decimal places our particular machine is capable of. If we had previously declared A to be of type INTEGER, however, we would be trying to assign a non-INTEGER value to an INTEGER variable, which would result in an error.

Pascal provides a way out of this unpalatable state of affairs by providing a couple of additional operators, known as DIV and MOD. To see what these two operators do, we will write a problem in division. Suppose someone asked us to divide 13 by 3. We would proceed like this:

$$\frac{4}{3)\overline{13}}\qquad \text{remainder 1}$$

Now suppose that we have three variables of type INTEGER—say A, B, and C. Let B := 13, and C := 3, and then write

A := B DIV C;

If we now WRITELN (A), we will find that A has the value of 4. That is, DIV has performed a division of integers and yielded an integer. The remainder of 1 is lost.

If we were to write this Pascal statement instead:

A := B MOD C;

and then WRITELN (A), we would find that A has the value of 1. In other words, MOD gives the *remainder* of the division.

On most machines, if X is of type REAL, and we write X := B/C, we will get 4.3333 . . . for X.

The following examples may be of some help in understanding the use of MOD and DIV.

Example

Evaluate the following expressions. You may assume that A, B, and C are of type INTEGER, and X is of type REAL.

Let B := 14;
    C := 7;
    A := 3;

What is the value of

A MOD B	(answer is 3)
B MOD A	(answer is 2)
A DIV B	(answer is 0)
B DIV A	(answer is 4)
X := B/A	(answer for X is 4.666 . . .)
X := A/B	(answer for X is 0.2142 . . .)
B := C/A	(error on most machines)
C := B/C	(error on most machines)
X := C/A	(answer for X is 2.333 . . .)

By these examples we discover that DIV and MOD are used only when integers are involved and the desired result is also to be an integer.

Finally in this section, we should mention a couple of the built-in features of Pascal. (There are several more that we will not discuss here.) The two functions in question are designed to either square a number or take its square root. Unfortunately, the functions look almost alike, and you may have to think a moment before you use them.

Suppose we have X and Y declared to be of type REAL, and that X := 27.2;
Then if we write

    Y := SQRT(X);

Y will have the value of 5.215 . . . , which is the square root of 27.2. If we write

    X := SQRT(81);

we will find that X is 9.0. Note that the operation SQRT always results in a REAL answer.

A built-in function that is easily confused with SQRT is SQR. SQR takes a number and multiplies it by itself. If the original number is of type INTEGER, then the answer also will be of type INTEGER. If the original number is of type REAL, then the answer will be of type REAL.

If we write X := SQR(9.1), we will get a value of 82.81 for X. If we write X := SQR(9.0), X will be 81.0. If we write X := SQR(9), we may get an error, since 9 is an integer and X is of type REAL. However, if we had declared A to be of type INTEGER, then we could indeed write A := SQR(9) without disaster, and we would find that A had a value of 81. (This result is installation dependent.)

There are several other built-in functions in Pascal. We will meet most of them in this text, and all of them are presented in the latter portion of Appendix A, if you just can't wait.

2.2.2 Begin and end

Pascal programs seem to be sprinkled liberally with the words BEGIN and END. There are two things to remember in this regard. First, for every BEGIN there must be an END. (The converse is not true: it is possible to have an END without a BEGIN.) Second, anything contained between a BEGIN and its corresponding END is treated as though it were a single statement.

If we have the following portion of a program:

```
BEGIN
        WRITE ('BILL');
        WRITE ('WALKER')
END;
```

the two statements between the BEGIN and END are treated as though they were a single statement. (Incidentally, the semicolons will be explained later.) We refer to this construction as a *compound statement*.

It is possible to "nest" statements like this:

```
BEGIN
        WRITE ('LINE 1');
        WRITE ('LINE 2');
        BEGIN
                WRITE ('LINE 3');
                WRITE ('LINE 4')
        END
END;
```

The result is a single compound statement which writes four items. This single statement is made up of *three* simpler statements, one of which is made up of *two* even more elementary statements!

Remember that a series of statements that are enclosed by BEGIN and END are treated as a single statement.

2.2.3 Statements and semicolons

As a general rule of thumb, we can state that *Pascal statements are separated one from the other by semicolons (;)*. A compound statement may be constructed out of several statements surrounded by BEGIN and END, but each statement within the block must end with a semicolon in order to separate it from the statement that follows it.

If you create a compound statement using BEGIN and END, it is *usually* necessary for the END to be followed by a semicolon, since it is the end of a statement (compound or otherwise).

There are a very few exceptions to this rule. We will meet them later in the book. The complete story is contained within Appendix A, if you are really in a hurry, but if you can wait, for now just remember that each Pascal statement, compound or otherwise, is separated from the statement following it by a semicolon.

A possible source of trouble. In some versions of Pascal, you will have a problem if the statement immediately before an END is followed by a semicolon. The resulting error message usually will be somewhat obscure, telling you "null statement not allowed" or somesuch. The remedies are simple. Either have the computer center get a version of Pascal which does not object to "null statements," or simply do not use the semicolon immediately before an END.

On systems which exhibit this trouble, the code

```
BEGIN
      WRITELN ('BILL')
END;
```

will work, while the code

```
BEGIN
      WRITELN ('BILL');
END;
```

will not work.

2.2.4   About indentations

The Pascal compiler does not recognize the presence or absence of indentations. It ignores them completely. Therefore, we can write our programs in a form which is readable to us, without regard to whatever form the machine might think is appropriate. We do not have to be careful to punch certain things in certain columns as we do with some other languages.

The two statements

```
BEGIN WRITE ('BILL') END;
```

and

```
BEGIN
      WRITE ('BILL')
END;
```

are equivalent. It is possible (though not desirable!) to write a complete Pascal program on a single line. We suggest that you adopt a reasonable method for making your programs readable. For instance, the author likes to cause corresponding BEGIN and END statements to line up vertically and the statements in between the BEGIN and END to be indented one or two spaces.

If a given program sequence can be made easier to read by proper indentation or by insertion of blank lines, then insert the lines or use the indentation. *The objective is readability, not the conservation of line numbers.*

2.2.5   Input and output the simple way

Pascal has several advanced features for writing or reading from various places, including the keyboard, printers, disk files, and other exotic options. For the moment, however, we are most interested in using Pascal to read things that we type on the keyboard and then to write the results of the program on the screen.

There are two statements that can be used for input to the program. They are: READ and READLN. We will discuss the difference between these two statements in a minute. It suffices to state that these two statements are used to enter (or "input") data into a program.

Two statements that can be used for output are: WRITE and WRITELN. As you might expect, there is a difference between these two statements that is similar to the difference between READ and READLN. We explore this difference below.

The statement WRITELN is known as the "write-line" statement. It causes the computer to write something on the screen and then *go to the next line.* There are times when one does not want to do this, and in those instances one uses the WRITE statement instead. We illustrate below, using only part of a whole program.

```
WRITE ('BILL');
WRITE ('WALKER');
WRITELN;
```

This will produce only one line of output, and then return to the beginning of the next line. The output will be

```
BILL WALKER
█
```

with the "blob" representing the position of the cursor on the screen. The statements

```
WRITE ('BILL');
WRITELN ('WALKER');
```

will cause the screen to show the same thing:

BILL WALKER
█

However, if I wrote this:

WRITE ('BILL');
WRITE ('WALKER');

I would get:

BILL WALKER█

Note where the "blob" is. Another WRITE or WRITELN would *continue* on the same line.[3]

We are able to summarize the difference between WRITE and WRITELN, then, by saying that WRITELN writes whatever it is supposed to and then goes to the next line, but WRITE writes whatever it is supposed to and then just sits there waiting for something else to be written.

Now, what about READ and READLN?

As you might guess, READ and READLN work a lot like WRITE and WRITELN, except that they are for reading values into the computer instead of having the computer write out values. Basically, READ will read something from a single line and then allow the next input to come from the same line. READLN will read something from a line and then go to the next line for the next input.

This sounds a little confusing, and unfortunately in some implementations of Pascal it has been carried out poorly, making for still more confusion. You may have to experiment a little with your machine, but here is how it is supposed to work.

Suppose that we want to type three numbers and have the machine write the sum of those numbers for us. There are several ways that we might want to do this problem. For instance, we might want to type one number to a line and hit the carriage return key after each number, so that the computer screen would look like this:

2
3
4
THE SUM IS 9

or we might wish to cause all of the input numbers to appear on one line, like this:

2 3 4
THE SUM IS 9

---

[3]Note to the advanced programmer: If the system buffer has been poorly implemented, it may require a WRITELN to cause the buffer to "dump" any output at all to the output device.

or we might even wish to put two of the input numbers on a single line and the third on a line by itself, like this:

```
2 3
4
THE SUM IS 9.
```

Of course, we have to write a program to add the three numbers together, but let's just concern ourselves with the appearance of the screen for the moment. You might guess that the differences in the appearance of the screen are from differences in the READ and READLN statements in the program. In this discussion, we will assume that we have previously arranged that A, B, and C are variables of type INTEGER, and we will ignore everything else in the program except the part that deals with input and output.

Return to the first example above for a moment, and suppose that we wish to type one number to a line, and hit the carriage return after each number, so that the computer screen looks like this:

```
2
3
4
THE SUM IS 9
```

(Just to have an example, we will suppose that you used the numbers 2, 3, and 4. You could have typed any three integers.)

The following segment of code will accomplish this task.

```
READLN(A);
READLN(B);
READLN(C);
WRITELIN ('THE SUM IS',A + B + C);
```

The READLN statements have taken input from the keyboard (or cards, or whatever) one line at a time and gone to the next line for the next item.

So what? Well, let's look at another example. Suppose we wanted to type three numbers, all on one line, and then have the computer give us the sum of those numbers. If we were watching the screen as we typed, we would want to see something like this:

```
2 3 4
THE SUM IS 9
```

(again assuming we chose to use 2, 3, and 4 as the numbers to type in.)

This code segment should accomplish this task:

```
READLN (A,B,C);
WRITELN ('THE SUM IS',A+B+C);
```

Now, what about the third example above, where we read two values from one line and a third value from a second line and then printed the sum?

There are several ways to do this, and here are some of them. All of these code segments do the same thing.

```
READLN (A,B);
READLN (C);
WRITELN ('THE SUM IS',A + B + C);
```

or

```
READ (A);
READLN (B);
READLN (C);
WRITELN ('THE SUM IS',A + B + C);
```

By examining these two code segments, we see that READ is the "moral equivalent" of WRITE and that READLN is the "moral equivalent" of WRI-TELN. That is, READ does not go to the next line to await the next value for input, but READLN does.

2.3   WRITING OUR FIRST SAMPLE PROGRAM

In this section, we will attempt to bring together all the things we have learned and write a sample program.

In order to outline carefully the problem that we are going to tackle, we will present it in five parts:

1. A careful definition of the problem. We surely can't solve the problem if we don't know exactly what it is.

2. An analysis of the problem. This will be a paragraph which describes our reasoning and thinking—not necessarily the program steps. This paragraph contains most of our creative musings.

3. A description of the flow of logic required to solve the problem. After we have analyzed the problem, then we are in a position to describe the logical steps to take to solve it.

4. The writing of the actual code. In this section, we put the results of the above efforts into practice and attempt to write a Pascal equivalent to paragraphs 2 and 3. *This step is done on paper, not on the machine.*

5. The actual code. Finally, we enter the code into the machine and run it.

Just to have a problem to do, we will assign ourselves the task of producing a Pascal program to write on the screen the letters of the alphabet from *A* through *Z*. Some of what follows will require some instinct from you. Learning to program a computer involves a lot of chickens and eggs. Alas! Just hold on—and be sure to duplicate each of these steps yourself.

In this section, we will attempt to write the program that we assigned ourselves above. We will follow the five-step process carefully.

The first step is *definition of the problem*.

2.3.1   Definition of the problem

We are assigned to write a Pascal program that will print on the screen the letters of the alphabet from *A* through *Z*. There will be no input from the keyboard, other than giving the instruction to execute. The output will be directed exclusively to the screen. We really should print a heading that describes what we are doing as well.

If we were doing a more elaborate program, this section would be more elaborate. But the objective of this section is to make it exceedingly clear to one and all, and especially ourselves, just what we expect the program to accomplish.

2.3.2   Analysis of the problem

We will define a variable called LETTER which takes on the values of the letters of the alphabet from *A* through *Z* and is written to the screen each time it assumes a new value. It is clear that LETTER will be a *variable* of type CHAR (for character).

Generating the previous (rather formidable) paragraph wasn't difficult, but understanding it is the important thing at this stage. Whether or not you could have done it yourself is not as important right now as whether you understand what it means. Again, we are encountering some chickens and eggs. Just hang tight—things get easier rather quickly now.

2.3.3   Description of the logic flow

Many different methods are used to describe the logic of a program. Some are more effective than others, but the goal of all of them should be to present the logic carefully and precisely to the person who is intending to write the program. It often helps (at least in your mind) to pretend that the person who is expected to write the actual program is not the same person as the one who decides *how* to write the program, and that the Description of Logic Flow is the method of communication between these two people. If you disallow all other methods of communication—including telephone, word of mouth, and pony express—then you begin to see just how carefully the Description of Logic Flow must be constructed.

For the problem at hand, it is helpful first to verbalize the program like this:

I will initialize the variable LETTER with the value A and print the value of LETTER. I will then assign the letter B to the variable LETTER and then again print LETTER. I will continue until LETTER attains the value of Z and it is printed, after which I will cease execution of the program.

This sentence describes in English the flow of logic of the program. At this stage in your study, you may have a hard time creating such a sentence, but you can probably understand the sentence as presented. Have faith—you are closer than you think!

2.3.4 Writing the code

We are now at the point where we must actually take computer in hand and write the program.

Now that we have completed these steps:

Definition of the Problem

Analysis of the Problem

Description of Logic Flow

we are ready to proceed with writing the program.

Let's examine the third step above more carefully. We can use it to help write the program in Pascal. By looking at the description of the logic flow, we can make a first attempt at writing our program, thus:

```
PROGRAM SAMPLE (INPUT,OUTPUT);
VAR:
BEGIN
      (*write the letters of the alphabet*)
END.
```

This program is obviously incomplete, but we do have the skeleton of a program. Almost all programs use variables of some type, and we have provided for a VAR section in our program. The main logic of the program will be contained between the BEGIN and END, although we have not yet defined exactly what it will look like.

In order to fill in the unfinished portions of our program, we must again turn our attention to the Description of Logic Flow.

We decided that we would "initialize the variable LETTER with the value A, and print the value of LETTER." Then, we ". . . assign the letter B to the variable LETTER and then again print LETTER."

We can accomplish this process by using the following code segment:

```
FOR LETTER : = 'A' TO 'Z' DO WRITELN (LETTER);
```

The FOR . . . DO . . . statement is further explained in section 4.3.4 of this text. For the moment, its use is somewhat instinctive. It may not have occurred to you to phrase it just that way, but perhaps you are able

to recognize what the code does, even though you might not have origi-
nated it yourself.

We observe that the variable LETTER must be included in the VAR section, and that LETTER is of type CHAR since it takes on values of letters of
the alphabet.

We put these considerations into the program in section 2.3.5, filling in
the portions that were unclear in the first attempt at writing the program.
See if it makes sense.

2.3.5 Using the code

```
PROGRAM SAMPLE (OUTPUT);
(* THERE ARE NO LABELS OR CONSTANTS, AND WE WILL USE
    ONLY THE STANDARD TYPES, SO LABEL, CONSTANT, AND
    TYPE DECLARATIONS ARE MISSING, AS ARE THE FUNCTION
    AND PROCEDURE DEFINITIONS *)
VAR LETTER : CHAR;
BEGIN (* THE START OF THE MAIN PROGRAM *)
    WRITELN (' THE LETTERS OF THE ALPHABET '); (* MAKES
    THE HEADING *)
    FOR LETTER : = 'A' TO 'Z' DO
        WRITELN (LETTER)
END. (* OF THE PROGRAM *)
```

This code follows the outline of the Description of Logic Flow that we
wrote above. There is absolutely no substitute for the experience of making
this program function correctly. By all means, stop now and load this program into your machine and run it. After it works, you might consider
changing some things. For instance, change the FOR LETTER : = 'A' TO
'Z' to something like FOR LETTER : = 'J' TO 'K' or even to FOR LETTER
: = '@' TO '0'. You might also change the WRITELN to WRITE and see
what happens.

The next section consists of examples and exercises. You have enough
Pascal at your disposal to accomplish all of the examples and exercises,
although you may have to ponder a while. Good luck!

2.4 EXAMPLES AND EXERCISES

Example 1

Write a program to sum the first 100 positive integers.

Definition of the problem

I am to write a program that will provide the sum of the first 100 positive integers. That is, I want to determine 1 + 2 + 3 + . . . + 100 and
write the answer.

Analysis

I will write a loop, using a FOR . . . DO . . . statement as in PRO-GRAM SAMPLE (see page 32). However, instead of writing something each time I go through the loop, I will just add a number to a total. Before I start adding numbers together, the total should be zero. After the numbers are added together, I will print the answer on the screen and end the program.

Description of logic flow

Before I start adding numbers together, the TOTAL is zero. I will arrange for a variable called NUMBER to take on the values of the whole numbers from 1 to 100, adding NUMBER to TOTAL each time NUMBER changes. After I have added 100 different numbers to TOTAL, I will print the value of TOTAL and end the program.

Writing the code

I will need at least two variables, one for the TOTAL and one for the NUMBER to be added to the TOTAL. Since both of these variables will have to hold only integers, they will be of type INTEGER.

After carefully studying PROGRAM SAMPLE, I should be able to write this program.

The code: Example one

```
PROGRAM EXAMPLE1(OUTPUT);
    VAR TOTAL,NUMBER : INTEGER;
    BEGIN
        TOTAL := 0; (* before I start, the total is zero *)
        FOR NUMBER := 1 TO 100 DO
            TOTAL := TOTAL + NUMBER;
        (* this "loop" lets NUMBER run from 1 to 100, adding it
            to TOTAL each time *)
        (* now it is time to output to the screen the TOTAL *)
        WRITELN ('THE SUM OF THE FIRST 100 INTEGERS IS',
            TOTAL)
    END. (* now end the program *)
```

By the way, the answer is 5,050. Try running this program to find the sum of the first 1,000 integers and see what you get.

The similarity to the PROGRAM SAMPLE is striking. Study this example until you understand it, since we will draw on your experience with this program and with the next two examples to allow you to do the exercises yourself.

Example 2

Write a program to write your name 276 times.

efinition of the problem

We are to write a Pascal program that will print a person's name on the screen 276 times.

Analysis

By simply saying "WRITELN ('Bill Walker')" I can cause "Bill Walker" to appear on the screen; so all I have to do is cause "WRITELN ('Bill Walker')" to be executed 276 times.

Description of logic flow

I will count the number of times that "Bill Walker" is written on the screen, using a variable called COUNT. The FOR . . . DO . . . looks like an easy way to solve this problem.

Writing the code

The only variable is COUNT. (My name never changes, so it is not a variable.)

The code looks like this:

```
PROGRAM EXAMPLE2(OUTPUT);
      VAR COUNT : INTEGER;
      BEGIN
            FOR COUNT := 1 TO 276 DO
                  WRITELN ('Bill Walker')
      END.
```

Hmmmmmmm. Maybe this Pascal stuff isn't so hard after all!

Example 3

Write a program to generate all two-letter words.

Definition of the problem

I am to write a program that will generate all the two-letter words that exist. However, I must decide just what a word is. Words such as *as* or *we* certainly count, but recognizing them as words depends upon extensive personal knowledge of the English language. For the sake of simplicity, we will agree to count *any* two-letter combination as a word. Thus, XX and CG are "words" for this program.

Analysis

All I have to do is write the letter *A* followed by each letter of the alphabet, then the letter *B* followed by each letter of the alphabet, and so on. In this way, I will write AA AB AC . . . AZ BA BB BC . . . BZ CA . . . and so on down to . . . ZX ZY ZZ.

Description of logic flow

I will use two variables, one for the first letter and one for the second letter. I will let the first letter take on the value A and then let the second letter take on all of the values from A to Z, writing the first letter and the second letter side by side each time. Then I will let the first letter take on the value of B and let the second letter run through all the values from A to Z again, and so on, until I have allowed all possible combinations of the first letter and the second letter to be printed.

Writing the code

I will need two variables, say, FIRST and SECOND, both of which will be of type CHAR since they are letters. I will put one FOR . . . DO . . . inside another FOR . . . DO. . . .

```
PROGRAM EXAMPLE3(OUTPUT);
    VAR FIRST,SECOND : CHAR;
    BEGIN
        FOR FIRST := 'A' TO 'Z' DO
            FOR SECOND := 'A' TO 'Z' DO
                WRITELN (FIRST,SECOND);
    END.
```

This program shows that it is possible to put one Pascal statement inside another one. The FOR . . . DO . . . loops are said to be *nested*.

Exercises

You have everything you need to write the following programs. You may need to refer to the preceding examples for ideas about how to do some things. Be sure to work these exercises, even though they may appear trivial.

1. Write a program to determine the product of the first 10 positive integers. Then try it for the first 100 positive integers. What happens? Why? Hint: Start the product at 1, *not* 0.

2. Generate all possible five-letter words, using FOR . . . DO . . . statements as in the examples above. A word is considered to be any five consecutive characters. Caution: Don't use the printer—there are 26^5 such words. (Write a program to determine how many that really is! The answer is about 36 boxes of paper.)

3. Write a program to read five numbers from the keyboard and provide their sum and product. Can you make one small change and then do the same thing for 50 numbers instead?

Stay with these until you get them working. Several modifications to the assigned problems may occur to you as you work them. Feel free to work additional problems if you want to. If you stop and "have fun" with the machine, you will probably be a better programmer for it.

3.0

Boolean algebra

3.1 BOOLEAN ALGEBRA

Before we study additional Pascal statements, we must digress and spend some time with a subject called *Boolean algebra*. This sounds formidable, but in reality it is a simple concept. The name *Boolean* is taken in honor of an English mathematician named George Boole. (His name rhymes with pool.)

In this chapter, we will study the notion of the relational operators, then learn how to form Boolean expressions by using the Boolean operators.

Plunge into Boolean algebra

All of this sounds pretty tough, but you can probably do it in the commercial breaks if you are watching TV. It only sounds tough. By the end of the chapter, you will be able to use Boolean algebra to your great advantage in writing programs, and you may even have discovered a new and entertaining party game!

If you are still worried about the concept of anything that contains the word *algebra,* take heart—it is possible to skip this chapter altogether without serious penalty. You may choose to return to study this chapter later. Like most other subjects, computer programming has a lot of "chicken and egg" problems in it. Those who are philosophically inclined may wish to read the present chapter and then decide whether it is an egg or a chicken.

3.2   WHAT IS BOOLEAN ALGEBRA?

Speaking simply, Boolean algebra involves performing operations with objects that can only take on two possible values. These values are known as *true* and *false.* We combine objects (which can have only two values) with other objects to form still other objects. In this section we will learn how to manipulate these objects.

We first define the concept of a *statement.* (This is going to be different from a Pascal language statement, so watch out.) A statement is a sentence, complete with subject and verb, that is either true or false but not both. Lest this sound silly, be aware that there are sentences (called paradoxes) which can be both. An example of a paradox is presented in Figure 3–1.

In Figure 3–1 we see both sides of the same index card, and the same thing is written on both sides. If you think about it for a minute, you may find it necessary to put this book up and go for a walk! At any rate, the definition of a statement is designed to rule out such paradoxes as the one shown in Figure 3–1.

Some examples of statements are:

Today is Monday.

Tomorrow will be Friday.

Yesterday was not Wednesday.

In the rest of this section we will learn how to form sentences (statements) written in the Pascal language. Each of these sentences will be ca-

Figure 3–1

| The statement on the other side is false. | The statement on the other side is false. |

pable of evaluation as either true or false (but not both), depending on their context, just as the above examples were.

3.3   BOOLEAN-VALUED EXPRESSIONS

We must first mention the relational operators. They are:

<	(is less than)
>	(is greater than)
=	(is equal to)
<=	(is less than or equal to)
>=	(is greater than or equal to)
<>	(is not equal to)

We will use these relational operators to help us define *Boolean expressions*. (Just hold on tight for a minute—the worst is already over.)

Boolean expressions are expressions which have only two possible values. These values are *true* and *false*. (For the moment, you can think of an expression as being about the same as a sentence in the English language.)

Suppose that we have the expression $8 < 10$. (It's a sentence in English if you read it aloud.) This expression is a true statement, so it has a Boolean value of TRUE. Some other statements, and their Boolean values are presented in Figure 3–2.

Whoops! Watch out!

If two variables are both of type INTEGER, or both of type REAL, or both of type CHAR, (or both of the same scalar type, which we will discuss later) we can use any of the relational operators to compare them.

However, if two variables are of different types, we can use only $=$ and $<>$ to compare them. The two variables must both be of the same type in order for *any* comparison to be legal, however.

Some implementations of Pascal (such as the popular UCSD version) allow all of the relational operators to be brought to bear on a nonstandard type known as STRING. This is not standard to the Pascal language.

Figure 3–2

Statement	Boolean value
A <= 10	TRUE
B <= A	TRUE
A < > C	FALSE
B >= C	FALSE
A <= A	TRUE

where we have made the assignments:
A := 7; B := 4; C := 7;

3.4 THE BOOLEAN OPERATORS

Just as we can combine several Pascal statements into a single compound statement (by use of BEGIN and END), we can also combine several Boolean expressions into a single Boolean expression by using the *Boolean operators*. These operators are: AND, OR, and NOT, and they are defined by the tables in Figure 3–3.

Figure 3–3

AND	TRUE	FALSE
TRUE	TRUE	FALSE
FALSE	FALSE	FALSE

OR	TRUE	FALSE
TRUE	TRUE	TRUE
FALSE	TRUE	FALSE

	TRUE	FALSE
NOT	FALSE	TRUE

The tables in Figure 3–3 tell how to compose simple Boolean expressions into compound Boolean expressions. Consider the first table:

		S2	
	AND	TRUE	FALSE
S1 TRUE		TRUE	FALSE
FALSE		FALSE	FALSE

This is called a *truth table*. It is used in this fashion: Suppose we have two Boolean-valued expressions (i.e., expressions that are either true or false but not both) labeled S1 and S2. S1 is described across the top line of the table, and S2 in the left-hand column. S is a third expression defined by S := S1 AND S2 (read it aloud). That is, we can find S at the intersection of the S1 column and the S2 line. We can thus conclude that

if S1 is TRUE and S2 is also TRUE, then S is TRUE
If S1 is FALSE and S2 is TRUE, then S is FALSE

We see that we can evaluate S for any combination of values for S1 and S2 by looking at the table.

In a similar fashion, if we are told that S := S1 OR S2, we can evaluate S for any combination of values for S1 and S2 by looking at the OR table in Figure 3–3.

Finally, we note that NOT changes the value of an expression to its opposite value.

As an exercise, suppose that S1 := TRUE, S2 := TRUE, and S3 := False, and then evaluate:

1.   SA = (S1 AND S2) OR (S1 AND S3)

2.   SB = S1 AND (S2 OR S1) AND S3

3.   Let S1 = "Cows give milk",
         S2 = "The sun comes up in the east," and
         S3 = "Mamma raccoons have three toes.",
     and then read SA and SB (in parts 1 and 2) in English.

4.   Assign SD := (S1 AND NOT S3) OR S3 and then evaluate SD (i.e.,
     is SD TRUE or FALSE).

It is possible to have assignment statements between Boolean-valued variables. We must declare the variables to be of type BOOLEAN in the VAR section of the program. Suppose that we have

     VAR S1, S2, S3 : BOOLEAN;

then the assignment

     S1 := (S2 OR S3) AND (S1)

is legal.

3.5   EXAMPLES AND EXERCISES

Example

Make the following assignments:

     A := 10;
     B := 7;
     C := 4;
     D := 10;

If we assign S as follows:

     S := (A = D) AND (B <> C)

then S is TRUE, but if we assign S by

     S := (A = D) AND (B = C)

then S is FALSE.

To see this, note that the first statement is the same as S := TRUE AND TRUE, which according to the truth table for AND yields a TRUE. The second statement is the same as S := TRUE AND FALSE, which according to the truth table for AND yields a FALSE.

If the AND operators are replaced by OR instead, then the first statement is S := TRUE OR TRUE, which according to the truth table for OR is

TRUE, and the second statement is S := TRUE OR FALSE, which according to the table is TRUE.

Exercises

1. Change the values of A, B, C, and D in the above example, and try it again.

2. Make these assignments:

   S1 := (A < 10)
   S2 := (B = 7)
   S3 := (B > A)
   S4 := S1 AND S2
   S5 := S1 OR S3
   S6 := S4 AND (NOT S2)

   Now let A := 5 and B := 8, and evaluate S1 through S6. Then let A := 9 and B := 8, and reevaluate S1 through S6 again.

3. Construct a parlor game by writing

   S1 := "Cows are green"
   S2 := "Mamma raccoons have three toes" (not true)
   S3 := "The sun comes up on the east side of town"

   and asking guests to evaluate

   (NOT (S1 AND S2)) OR ((NOT S3) AND S1)

   Ask them to write this sentence in English!

4.0

Chapter 4

The control statements

4.1   INTRODUCTION

In this section we will discuss five Pascal statements:

```
IF . . . THEN . . . ELSE . . .
WHILE . . . DO . . .
REPEAT . . . UNTIL . . .
FOR . . . DO . . .
CASE . . . OF . . .
```

Each of these statements involves taking an action contingent upon a condition being met. These statements provide much of the power and simplicity of the language and allow us to write meaningful programs.

The control structures

When combined with assignment statements, these statements provide us with a rich assortment of programming constructions.

The presence of these five statements is what makes the GO TO statement almost obsolete in Pascal. We will discuss each in turn.

At the beginning of this book, we promised that we would soon begin to construct "building blocks", which would form the elements we would use to write Pascal programs. The five control structures mentioned above are the most fundamental of these building blocks. By proper application of these structures, we will soon be able to write rather large and complex programs with comparative ease.

4.2   THE IF . . . THEN . . . ELSE . . . STATEMENT

Suppose that I were to say, "If my clock goes off, then I will get up; otherwise, I'll sleep late." This is an expression of a *conditional*. I can represent it graphically, as in the figure below.

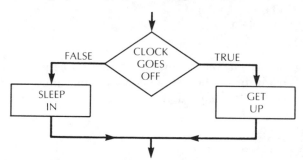

The IF . . . THEN . . . ELSE . . . statement allows me to choose one of two possible courses of action depending on whether or not a given condition is met.

The Pascal version of this concept appears in the language as

IF CONDITION THEN STATEMENT1 ELSE STATEMENT2;

and is interpreted graphically as in the following figure.

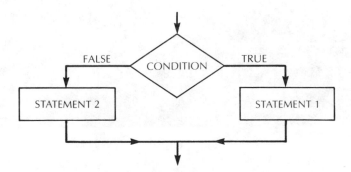

If the condition is true, then STATEMENT1 is executed; if the condition is not true, then STATEMENT2 is executed. Statements 1 and 2 can be any legal Pascal statements, including compound statements constructed by use of BEGIN and END.

What can we put in place of CONDITION? The answer is, any Boolean-valued expression. Those readers who skipped Chapter 3 may be comforted by the fact that a CONDITION is often something like X = 6 or perhaps C <= D.

4.3   THE WHILE . . . DO . . . STATEMENT

The form of the Pascal WHILE . . . DO . . . is

WHILE CONDITION DO SOMETHING;

and is interpreted by the sentence, "So long as the condition is true, do the SOMETHING." We expect that the SOMETHING—which may of course be a simple or compound statement—will eventually affect the status of the CONDITION.

Graphically, the WHILE . . DO . . . can be represented by the flow-chart below. Again, the CONDITION may be any Boolean expression, compound or not.

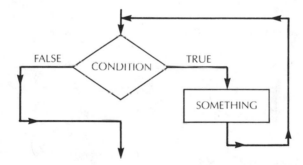

Consider the following block of code:

```
INDEX : = 1;
WHILE INDEX <= 100 DO
      BEGIN
            WRITE (INDEX);
            INDEX := INDEX + 1;
      END;
```

Can you predict the result? What will be the last number written? If I reverse the order of the WRITE and assignment statements, what will be the last number written? What is the final value of INDEX in each case?

Now consider this block of code:

```
INDEX := 1000;
WHILE INDEX <= 100 DO
    BEGIN
        WRITE(INDEX);
        INDEX: = INDEX + 1;
    END;
```

What is the last number written? What is the value of INDEX after the code has been executed?

One of the nicest things about the WHILE . . . DO . . . construction is that the condition is tested BEFORE the statement is executed. If the condition is not true, the statement is not executed at all. This is not the case, however, with another Pascal construction known as the REPEAT . . . UNTIL. . . .

4.4   THE REPEAT . . . UNTIL . . . STATEMENT

The Pascal syntax of this construction is

REPEAT STATEMENT UNTIL CONDITION;

and it is interpreted by the sentence, "Repeat the statement until the condition is true." This construction can be represented graphically by the following flowchart. It is important to note that the test of the condition takes place *after* the statement has been executed.

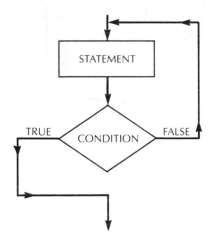

Consider the following code:

```
INDEX := 1;
REPEAT
        BEGIN
            WRITE (INDEX);
```

                         INDEX := INDEX + 1
                    END;
                  UNTIL INDEX = 100;

What will be the last number printed? What will be the value of INDEX after the program has been executed? What will be the output of the program if we reverse the order of the WRITE and the assignment? What if the original INDEX := 1 is replaced by INDEX := 1000?

Can you state the major difference between WHILE . . . DO . . . and REPEAT . . . UNTIL . . . ?

4.5   THE FOR . . . DO . . . STATEMENT

The FOR . . . DO . . . statement is designed to repeat a segment of code a certain number of times. It has some idiosyncracies.

A Pascal statement using FOR . . . DO . . . is:

    FOR LOOPVARIABLE := START TO FINISH DO STATEMENT;

LOOPVARIABLE must be of *enumerated type* (which is explained in Chapter 6). It takes an initial value of START, and the STATEMENT is executed, increasing LOOPVARIABLE by one each time through the loop, until LOOPVARIABLE attains the value of FINISH.

The FOR . . . DO . . . can be made to run backwards by substituting the word DOWNTO in place of the word TO. In this case, LOOPVARIABLE is *decreased* by one each time through the loop. Examples of FOR . . . DO . . . statements that run forwards and backwards are:

    FOR INDEX := 1 TO 100 DO WRITE (INDEX);
    FOR VALUE := 1000 DOWNTO 100 DO WRITE (INDEX);

By the way, DOWNTO is a single word, not two words!

FOR . . . DO . . . loops are frequently abused. They are intended to be used as counting loops. That is, they are used when you know *exactly* how many times a given loop is to be executed. No "stepsize" other than 1 is available. Actually, as we will discover in a later chapter, we can "step" through the members of any enumerated type, but for the present, the reader can consider that FOR . . . DO . . . loops can step through the integers.

4.6   THE CASE . . . OF . . . STATEMENT

The CASE statement is one of the most powerful constructs in Pascal. Suppose that CH is any variable of an enumerated type. (INTEGER and CHAR are legal, among others.) As an example, suppose that type LETTER

= 'A' . . 'Z', and suppose that CH is of type LETTER. Then the following code is both legal and useful.

```
CASE CH OF
        'A', 'E', 'I', 'O', 'U' : X := 6;
        'X', 'Y', 'Z' : X := 10;
    END;
```

If CH has as its value one of the vowels, the statement X := 6 will be executed. If CH is 'X', 'Y' or 'Z', then X := 10 is executed. Note that the CASE statement can be used like a number of nested IF . . . THEN . . . ELSE . . . statements.

There are several other things to note as well. The END that concludes the CASE statement has no matching BEGIN. This is rather unusual in Pascal, so it is a situation of note.

Another question that one must be aware of is this: What if the value of CH is 'M'? What will the CASE statement do then? We hope that it will not do anything. Unfortunately, some versions of Pascal simply "blow up" the program if the value of CH is not matched. One can provide a guardian statement above the CASE statement to ensure that CH is always properly defined. One easy way to do this is to make use of SET types, which we will discuss later.

A final note: The semicolon *before* the END statement above is redundant and could be left out.

The flowchart in Figure 4–1 illustrates the effect of using the CASE statement above.

4.7   COMMENTARY ON STRUCTURING PROGRAMS

At this point it might be a good idea to turn back to Chapter 1 of this book and reread sections 1.3, 1.4, and 1.5. As you recall, these sections dealt with the notion that programs should be built out of building blocks, which were represented by boxes that had single entry and single exit points. In Chapter 1 we pointed out that Pascal lends itself nicely to structured programming.

If you will refer to Figure 4–2, where we have presented once again the Pascal control structures in flowchart form, you will observe that each control structure can be placed in a dotted box that has only a single entry and a single exit. Herein, then, is the crux of the matter: Pascal control structures are single-entry, single-exit structures, so that they can form the building blocks necessary to true top-down structured programming. The output of one control structure can be fed into another control structure with the assurance that each has exactly one entrance and exactly one exit.

Figure 4–1
The CASE . . . OF . . . statement illustrated

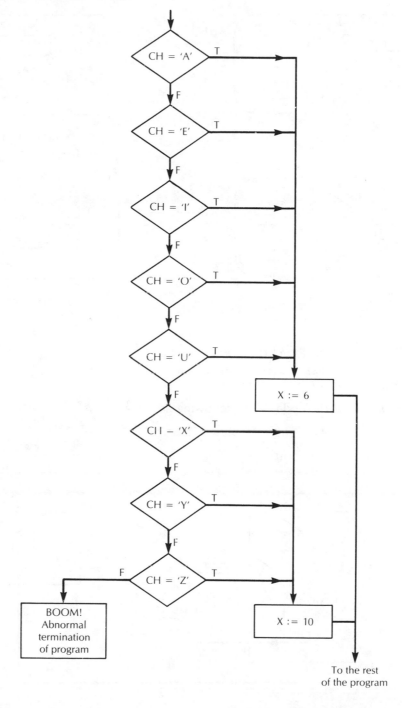

To the rest
of the program

Figure 4–2

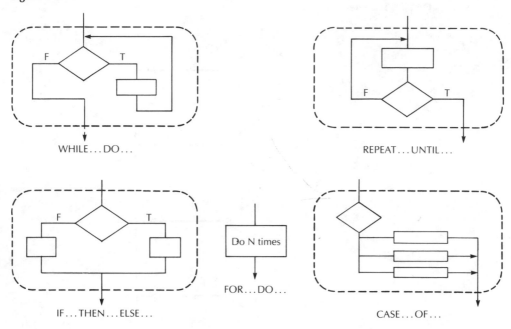

WHILE...DO...   REPEAT...UNTIL...

IF...THEN...ELSE...   FOR...DO...   CASE...OF...

4.8   EXAMPLES AND EXERCISES

Example 1

Write code for the following flowchart:

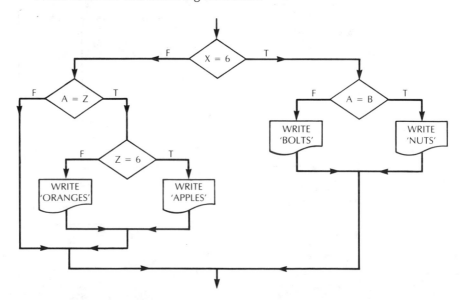

Answer:

```
IF X = 6 THEN
        IF A = B THEN
                WRITE ('NUTS')
        ELSE
                WRITE ('BOLTS')
ELSE
        IF A = Z THEN
                IF Z = 6 THEN
                        WRITE ('APPLES')
                ELSE
                        WRITE ('ORANGES'):
```

Note the lack of semicolons.

Example 2

Flowchart the following code:

```
IF A = B THEN
        IF (Q = S) THEN
                BEGIN
                        WRITE ('THIS');
                        R := 16;
                END
        ELSE
                IF T = U THEN
                        WRITE ('U = T');
```

The correct flowchart is shown below.

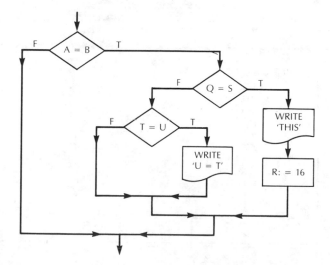

Example 3

Show three methods for writing the whole numbers from 1 to 100.

Solution 1

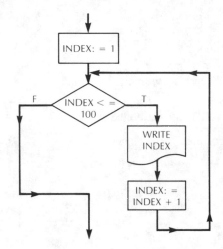

The code for Solution 1 is as follows:

```
INDEX: = 1;
WHILE INDEX <= 100 DO
    BEGIN
        WRITELN (INDEX);
        INDEX := INDEX + 1
    END;
```

Solution 2

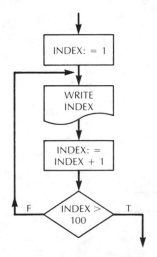

The code for Solution 2 is as follows:

```
INDEX := 1;
REPEAT
     WRITELN (INDEX);
     INDEX := INDEX + 1
UNTIL INDEX > 100;
```

Solution 3

Solution 3 consists of this code:

```
FOR INDEX: = 1 TO 100
     DO WRITELN (INDEX);
```

Exercises

1. Write a program to determine the product of the first 10 positive whole numbers. That is, determine $1 \cdot 2 \cdot 3 \cdot 4 \cdot 5 \cdot 6 \cdot 7 \cdot 8 \cdot 9 \cdot 10$. This can be done using brute force, or by using WHILE . . . DO . . ., or REPEAT . . . UNTIL . . ., or FOR . . . DO . . . statements. Try for all of these.

2. Write a program that will act as a simple cash register, producing taxable and nontaxable totals and a grand total. This program can be elaborated considerably, and it is presented in Chapter 10 in a usable form. This can be a challenging problem. The diagram should give you a big hint.

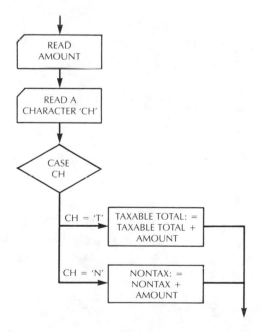

3.   Write a program that will accept a series of numbers, ending with the
     number 0, and then produce the sum and average of the numbers.
     The diagram should help you.

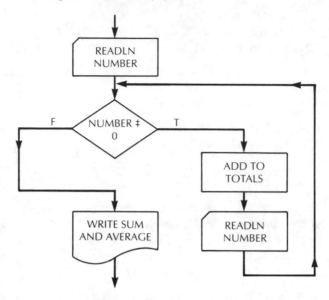

5.0

Procedures and functions

5.1   SOLVING THROUGH SIDETRACKS

In this chapter, we will meet the concept of a *subprogram*. This concept, perhaps more than any other, enables us to write readable Pascal programs.

If you have ever programmed before (or even if you haven't), you are probably aware that in the course of working a problem you sometimes need to break off from the main task, go off to the side and perform a related task, and then continue with the first task, using the results of the side calculation to aid in completion of the original job. In Pascal, such side calculations are known as *subprograms*. (Some other computer languages call them subroutines.)

There are two main kinds of Pascal subprogram: *procedures* and *func-*

Easy—just invoke the procedure

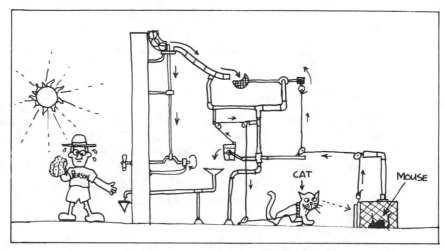

tions. *Functions* are subprograms that return exactly one value to the calling program, while *procedures* are subprograms that may return as many or as few values as desired to the main program.

When we execute either one, all we are actually doing is jumping off to the side (to a subprogram) to perform some task, and then returning to the main program to continue with the original job. This chapter has two main subjects: how to write a subprogram, and how to cause the main program to communicate effectively with the subprogram.

After you have read this chapter (and worked the examples!) you will be able to write Pascal programs that make use of procedures and functions and that are considerably more readable than some of the programs that you had written before. We encourage you to study this chapter carefully. The benefits are well worth the effort.

5.2   CONCEPT OF A SUBPROGRAM

Suppose that I desire to solve the following problem.

I am buying pizzas and love mushroom pizza. If I am able to acquire mushroom topping on a pizza, I always buy one eight-inch pizza. But if I can't have mushrooms, I always buy two five-inch pizzas. Assuming that all pizzas are one inch thick, what is the volume of pizza that I consume in either instance?

I write the following program segment to solve this problem.

```
        .
        .
        .
IF TOPPING = MUSHROOM THEN
        VOLUME : = PI * 4 * 4
ELSE
     BEGIN
        VOLUME : = PI * 2.5 * 2.5;
        VOLUME : = VOLUME *2;
     END;
   WRITELN (VOLUME);
```

I observe that in two of the program segment's lines, I have made essentially the same calculation, that of multiplying the radius squared by the value of PI (which I probably defined in the CONST section.) In principal, I am repeating a code segment, although with different numbers involved.

Now consider the following code. (TYPE and VAR sections are omitted for clarity, as is a part of the program that would probably initialize the variables.)

```
PROGRAM EATS (INPUT, OUTPUT);
PROCEDURE COMPUTEVOLUME (R: INTEGER);
```

```
        BEGIN
            VOLUME: = PI * R * R;
        END;
    BEGIN (*MAIN PROGRAM*)
        IF TOPPING = MUSHROOM THEN
                COMPUTEVOLUME (4)
        ELSE
            BEGIN
                COMPUTEVOLUME (2.5);
                VOLUME := VOLUME * 2;
            END;
        WRITELN (VOLUME);
    END.
```

In this program segment, the repeated calculation has been replaced by a *procedure* which can take any radius and compute the corresponding volume of the pizza. The advantages are several; if computing volume were more complicated, they would be obvious. In any event, the readability of the program has been somewhat improved. (That is a matter of personal opinion, however.)

Both procedures (and functions) come *before* the main body of the program. In the procedure above, the value of R was communicated from the main body of the program to the procedure, and the value of VOLUME was communicated back from the procedure to the main program.

5.3   COMMUNICATION OF VARIABLES

Variables must be communicated between procedures or functions and the main program. This communication can take place in four main ways, depending on the programmer's preference. Variables can be:

1.   Global variables.

2.   Local variables.

3.   Pass by reference.

4.   Pass by value.

Each of these is discussed in a section below. Although our examples will use procedures, most of the following applies equally well to functions. Functions will be discussed in section 5.4.

5.3.1   Global variables

Consider the two boxes below. The box labeled MAIN is considered to be a Pascal main program that calls for a procedure named BOX.

MAIN PROCEDURE BOX;

```
.
.
.
VAR A, B: INTEGER;
.
.
.
A := 1;
B := 2;
WRITELN (A,B);
BOX;
WRITELN (A,B);
.
.
.
```

```
.
.
.
WRITELN (A,B);
A := 3;
B := 4;
.
.
.
```

The result of running this program will be:

```
1       2
1       2
3       4
```

In other words, the variables A and B have the same meaning in each box. A change in the value of either A or B within one of the boxes is reflected in the other box. Variables treated in this fashion are called *global variables*.

5.3.2   Local variables

We now consider the case where variables mentioned in one part of a particular program have no relation whatsoever to variables by the same name in another part of the program. Again, study the two boxes below.

MAIN PROCEDURE BOX;

```
.
.
.
VAR A, B: INTEGER;
.
.
.
A := 1;
B := 2;
WRITELN (A,B);
BOX;
WRITELN (A,B);
.
.
.
```

```
.
.
.
VAR A, B: INTEGER;
.
.
.
A := 3;
B := 4;
WRITELN (A,B);
.
.
.
```

The result of running this program will be:

```
1        2
3        4
1        2
```

We see that the variables A and B in the main portion of the program bear no relation at all to the same variables in the procedure. A change in these variables is *local* to the portion of the program that created the variable in the first place. Local variables have a great deal of application when one wants to be sure that unwanted "side effects" are not caused by inclusion of a particular procedure or function.

5.3.3   Pass by reference

Pass by reference is the usual FORTRAN method of handling subroutine parameters. It makes use of "dummy" variables. We will consider first the boxes below:

| | **PROCEDURE BOX** |
| **MAIN** | **(VAR X,Y: INTEGER);** |

```
VAR A, B: INTEGER;          .
   .                        .
   .                        .
   .                        .
   .                        WRITELN (X,Y);
A := 1; B := 2;             X := 3;
WRITFI N (A,B);             Y := 4;
Box (A,B);                  .
WRITELN (A,B);              .
   .                        .
   .
   .
```

The result of the WRITELN statements will be:

```
1        2
1        2
3        4
```

This output indicates that the values of A and B in the main program were somehow communicated to the procedure section, where they became the values of X and Y. Moreover, the changes in the values of X and Y were then reflected in corresponding changes in the values of A and B in the main program.

In this case, X and Y are dummy variables in the procedure, and they take their values in the procedure from the order of their placement in the calling line. Note the difference in the heading of the procedure, and in the calling line. This method of communication is called *pass by reference* since an actual address of a variable is passed back and forth, and not the contents of the address. That is, the address of the variable A in the main program is communicated to the procedure section, where it becomes the address of the variable X.

Now consider this set of boxes:

| | PROCEDURE BOX |
| MAIN | (VAR X, Y: INTEGER); |

```
.                                          .
.                                          .
.                                          .
VAR A, B, X, Y: INTEGER;                   WRITELN (X,Y);
.                                          X := 3;
.                                          Y := 4;
.                                          .
A := 1; B := 2;                            .
X := 8; Y := 9;                            .
Box (A,B);
WRITELN (A,B);
WRITELN (X,Y);
.
.
.
```

The output of this program setup will be:

```
1       2
3       4
8       9
```

From this example we realize that the X and Y in the procedure are *totally independent* of the X and Y in the main program. That is, the changes in the values of X and Y that were made in the procedure were *not* reflected as changes in X and Y in the main program. The variables that *did* have their values changed were those variables that were between the parentheses in the BOX(A,B) calling statement.

The main use of pass by reference is to establish a two-way communication of values between the main program and a procedure. Pass by reference defines a rather narrow "street" for these values to follow on their journey. The key to recognizing pass by reference is the presence of the VAR in the procedure heading.

5.3.4   Pass by value

Pass by value does not communicate the address of a variable as pass by reference does. Rather, pass by value communicates the actual contents of the address—i.e., the actual value of that parameter.

PROCEDURE BOX
MAIN   (X, Y: INTEGER);

```
.                         .
.                         .
.                         .
VAR A,B: INTEGER;         WRITELN (X,Y);
.                         X = 3;
.                         Y := 4;
.                         .
A := 1;                   .
B := 2;                   .
BOX (A,B);
WRITELN (A,B);
.
.
.
```

The (perhaps surprising) output of this will be

1   2
1   2

The values of A and B are communicated *to* the procedure, but the values of X and Y do not replace the values of A and B. Note the subtle difference in the procedure heading. (No VAR.)

We used the analogy of a two-way street when discussing pass by reference. Pass by value is like a one-way street. The values of variables are communicated *into* the procedure, but *not* back to the main program.

The key to recognizing pass by value is the absence of the VAR in the procedure heading.

5.3.5   Avoiding miscommunication

The reader may ask at this point *why* so many different mechanisms are available in Pascal for passing the values of variables back and forth between main programs and procedures or functions. The complete answer lies in a notion called *scope,* which we will ignore for the most part in this text. Instead, we present an example that may show that variables in the main program and variables in procedures can sometimes interact in unexpected (and disastrous) ways.

Suppose that we are asked to write the integers from 1 to 10, repeated 50 times. Let us design a procedure that writes the integers from 1 to 10, and then call that procedure 50 times. For clarity, we have left off quite a bit of the following program and presented only the parts which illustrate the point that we are trying to make.

```
PROGRAM . . .
      .
    VAR I : INTEGER;
      .
    PROCEDURE PUTNUMBERS;
        BEGIN
            FOR I := 1 TO 10 DO
                    WRITELN (I)
        END;
      .
      .

    BEGIN (* MAIN *)
        FOR I := 1 TO 50 DO
                PUTNUMBERS
    END.
```

If we run this program, we will find a disastrous interaction between I in the procedure and I in the main program. This interaction could have been avoided by making I local to the procedure—i.e., by including VAR I : INTEGER; right after the procedure heading. (In parentheses, of course.)

As a general rule, if a variable is to be communicated to a procedure, and that procedure is not explicitly intended to change the variable, then we should use pass by value to communicate the variable. The only variables that should be passed by reference are those variables that will have their values changed by the procedure and, furthermore, *whose changed values need to be reflected in the main program.*

An even sterner rule is useful: Keep all variables as local as possible. For instance, if you use I as the index of a FOR . . . DO . . . loop in a procedure, you want to be sure that you don't inadvertently let it interact with I in some other procedure, or with I used in a different fashion in the main program. The way to prevent this is to make I a local variable in the procedure.

The only communication paths between a procedure and the main program should be those paths which you, the programmer, have specifically provided. These paths may be one way or two way, as you will, but they should be under your control. To maximize your control, global variables should be the exception rather than the rule in Pascal programs.

Just for fun, when you write your next Pascal program that uses procedures (or functions, of course), see whether you can minimize the communication of variables between the subprogram and the main program. You will want to make maximum use of local variables and carefully apply pass-by-reference and pass-by-value concepts. Chances are that the result will be an unusually "clean" and functional program.

5.4   FUNCTION SUBPROGRAMS

Most of the discussion so far has dealt with procedures, not functions (although we did meet some built-in Pascal functions very early in the text). As you will recall, functions are subprograms that return exactly one value to the calling program, while procedures are subprograms that may return as many or as few values as desired to the main program. At first glance, functions would seem to have little use, if procedures are capable of doing the same things with more flexibility. It turns out that each type of subprogram has its place, however.

Suppose that we are to write a program statement that will accept the two sides of a right triangle and return the length of the hypotenuse. We grant that writing a subprogram to accomplish this task may be a case of "shooting a mouse with a cannon," but as an illustration it will serve.

If we write a procedure to perform the operations of squaring the two sides, adding them together, taking the square root of the sum, and returning that value to the main program, it might look something like this:

```
PROCEDURE HYPOT (X,Y:REAL; VAR Z: REAL);
    BEGIN
            Z := SQRT (X*X + Y*Y)
    END;
```

Now, if somewhere in our program we were asked to give the total length of the hypotenuses for two different triangles, we could write the following code segment:

```
    .
    .

HYPOT (X1,Y1,Z1);
HYPOT (X2,Y2,Z2);
TOTAL := Z1 + Z2;
WRITELN (TOTAL);
    .
    .
```

Since this seems awkward, let's consider whether a function might be an improvement. We recall that a function can return exactly one value to the calling program. It turns out that the foreknowledge that there will be exactly one value returned allows Pascal to work with functions a little differently.

Let us write:

```
FUNCTION HYPOT (X,Y : REAL) : REAL;
    BEGIN
```

```
                 HYPOT := SQRT(X*X + Y*Y);
         END;
```

Now, our program segment above could be written like this:

```
     .

     .

     TOTAL := HYPOT(X1,Y1) + HYPOT (X2,Y2);
     WRITELN (TOTAL);
     .

     .
```

or even just

```
     WRITELN (HYPOT(X1,Y1) + HYPOT (X2,Y2));
```

We see from this example that we can use functions wherever we could use a single number (or a single variable). It is legal to perform arithmetic with the results of functions. Consider an example that uses two of Pascal's built-in functions:

```
     Z := SQRT(SQR(X) + SQR(Y));
```

This program statement calls SQR twice on a single line and calls SQRT once.

Note that writing functions differs from writing procedures in a couple of ways. The first difference to strike us appears on the first line of the function. For example, in the function defined below, the word REAL appears on the first line. This tells the computer that the result of the function is expected to be a REAL number. If we had expected the result to be of type INTEGER, we would have put INTEGER in place of the word REAL. Most versions of Pascal allow only REAL, INTEGER, CHAR, and BOOLEAN results for functions along with a type called POINTER that we will study later. A very few versions allow other types as well.

Our example function is:

```
     FUNCTION HYPOT(X,Y:REAL):REAL;
         BEGIN
                 HYPOT := SQRT(X*X + Y*Y);
         END;
```

Of course we notice that the word PROCEDURE has been replaced by the word FUNCTION, but there is yet another difference. *The name (HYPOT) of the function appears in the body of the function, and on the left side of an assignment operator.*

Finally, we should note that Pascal has many built-in functions, including functions for determining trigonometric and other arithmetic quantities. These are summarized in Appendix A.

5.5 EXAMPLES AND EXERCISES

Example 1

All the methods described so far can be combined into a single program. You should play with the following program until you understand it.

```
PROGRAM EXAMPLE (OUTPUT);
    var A, B, C, D, J: INTEGER;
    PROCEDURE FIXIT (X, Y: INTEGER; VAR Z,W: INTEGER);
        VAR C, D: INTEGER;
        BEGIN
            WRITELN (X, Y, Z, W, J);
            X := 7; Y := 8, Z := 9; W := 10; J := 18;
                C := 14; D := 16;
            WRITELN (X, Y, Z, W, J, C, D);
        END;
    BEGIN
        A := 1; B := 2; C := 3; D := 4; J := 12;
        WRITELN (A, B, C, D, J);
        FIXIT (A, B, C, D);
        WRITELN (A, B, C, D, J);
    END.
```

The output will be:

1	2	3	4	12		
1	2	3	4	12		
7	8	9	10	18	14	16
1	2	9	10	18		

Example 2

Run the following code, and try to decide why the program does not work.

```
PROGRAM ONE (OUTPUT);
        VAR INDEX: INTEGER;
    PROCEDURE WRITIT (VAR INDEX: INTEGER);
        BEGIN
            INDEX := 20;
            WRITELN (INDEX)
        END;
    BEGIN
        FOR INDEX := 1 TO 10 DO
```

WRITIT (INDEX)
END.

Answer

INDEX in the procedure is causing INDEX in the FOR loop always to be 20. This causes an error. The solution is to replace PROCEDURE WRITIT (VAR INDEX: INTEGER) with PROCEDURE WRITIT (INDEX: INTEGER). You will also have to eliminate the line that sets INDEX := 20;.

Example 3

Write a program to compute the sum of the averages of the numbers $1 + 0, 1 + 1, 1 + 2, 1 + 3, 1 + 4, \ldots, 1 + 10$.

```
PROGRAM FUNNY(INPUT,OUTPUT);
    VAR I : INTEGER; SUM : REAL;
    FUNCTION AVE (A,B : INTEGER) :REAL;
        BEGIN
            AVE := (A + B) / 2;
        END;
    BEGIN (* main program *)
        SUM := 0.0;
        FOR I := 1 TO 10 DO
            SUM := SUM + AVE(1,I);
        WRITELN (SUM);
    END.
```

In this example we notice that variables being passed *to* the function can be passed by value. In truth, they can be passed by reference as well, and a function can also make use of global and local variables. We remark again that this should be done with care, to prevent unwanted interaction with other parts of the program.

Exercise

1. Make a "check writer" program. Use a procedure that accepts a number like $127.60 and writes "one hundred twenty-seven dollars and sixty cents." This will involve several CASE . . . OF . . . statements. Make the main program look something like the code at the top of the next page.

```
READLN (AMOUNT);
WHILE AMOUNT >= 0 DO
    BEGIN
        PRINTCHECK (AMOUNT);
        READLN (AMOUNT)
    END;
```

Assume that AMOUNT will be <= $1,000, for simplicity's sake.

2. Make a simple "clock" that will "beep" every 10 seconds. *Hint:* Use a stopwatch to see how long your computer takes to perform procedure DELAY.

```
PROCEDURE DELAY;
  BEGIN
    N = 1000;
    FOR I := 1 TO N DO
        BEGIN
            X := (1/2 * 3 * 98.61 *427/980/9801 * 9801)
        END;
  END;
```

Then adjust N so that DELAY takes 10 seconds.

Now try

```
DONE := FALSE;
WHILE NOT DONE DO
    BEGIN
        DELAY;
        WRITELN (CI IR (7)); (* THIS RINGS THE BELL*)
    END;
```

How can you make "fine adjustments" to the clock? *Note:* This entire exercise is probably futile on time-sharing computers.

3. Write a program that will read a worker's identification number (IDNO), hourly rate of pay, and number of hours worked during a week. Have the machine write a report giving identification number, number of hours worked, regular pay, overtime pay, and total pay.

    Do this until an IDNO of 0000 is encountered. Count as overtime anything over 40 hours, and be sure to pay time and a half for overtime. *Hint:* Write functions for computing regular pay and overtime pay, and use them as follows:

```
        .
        .
        .

TOTAL : = 0;
    READLN (IDNO);
        WHILE IDNO <> 0 DO
            BEGIN
                READLN (HOURS, RATE);
                TOTAL : =  REG(HOURS) +
                    OVER(HOURS);
                WRITELN (IDNO, RATE, HOURS,
                    REG (HOURS), OVER (HOURS),
                    TOTAL);
                READLN (IDNO);
            END;
        .
        .
        .
```

6.0

Chapter 6

Using types

6.1 STRONG TYPING: BLESSING OR CURSE?

Each time we have discussed a new feature of Pascal, we have claimed that that particular feature sets Pascal off from many other programming languages. Lest we be accused of repetition, we must state unequivocally that *many* features of Pascal are unique, and *many* features of Pascal set it off from other languages. The harmonious interaction of these unique features is what makes Pascal the uniquely powerful language that it is.

One of the most important features of Pascal is its *strong typing*. This does not mean that a strong hand is required to run the keyboard. As you will recall, all variables possess certain attributes that constitute TYPE and *strong typing* means that Pascal checks these attributes more carefully than some other languages do. This can be a blessing or a curse, depending on your attitude. (The programmer must take great care not to combine objects of different type frivolously.)

We take the attitude that strong typing is a blessing, because it can save us from ourselves when we write one thing and mean another. Eventually, we will learn to define our own types—that is, we will decide on a set of attributes for an object to possess and force that object to possess those attributes.

This chapter will give a first look at the concept of type and acquaint us with the notion of building nonstandard types from standard ones. Later chapters will enhance our abilities along these lines.

One of the "neatest" things about the notion of type is that it can lead to some very "fun" and interesting applications. Enjoy!

6.2 THE NOTION OF TYPE

We have discovered that Pascal, like most other computer languages, stores numbers differently depending upon the presence or absence of a decimal point. We also know that alphabetic information (ie items of type CHAR) is stored in yet a different fashion.

Each TYPE is a set of objects that share a certain characteristic. For instance, we have previously defined the type INTEGER to consist of all of the whole numbers (that is, numbers which can be expressed without decimal points). Type REAL, on the other hand, consists of numbers which do contain decimal points. (A mathematician would take exception to this definition, but historically it must stand.) Type CHAR comprises alphabetic information, and type BOOLEAN is made of the objects TRUE and FALSE.

If we are given an entity, say a 2, it is easy to decide that this entity has all the characteristics of the type known as INTEGER and so it must *belong to* the type INTEGER. In a like manner, if the number 3.14 turns up, we can, by inspecting the definition of REAL, determine that this object is of type REAL. The same observation holds for objects of types BOOLEAN and CHAR. Moreover, any given object can belong to, at most, *one* of these types. That is, there is no object which belongs to more than one type.

However, it is clear that—in the human world at least—there are lots of objects which do not fit into any of these predefined categories. For instance, Saturday is a day of the week; it does not fit any of the types above. Nevertheless, we might very well want to have the computer deal with an object called Saturday if we happen to be writing a program to compute payrolls for our business.

It is the purpose of this chapter to expand on the definition of type to the point that we can invent our own types. It is no more absurd for the machine to deal with the entity Saturday than it is for the machine to deal with an entity named 2.34.

As an introduction to the notion of type, we will work our way through an example which may help us expand our abilities considerably and may even be fun besides!

6.3   INTRODUCTION TO DEFINING TYPES

Suppose someone confronts us with the following problem: write a program that will read an employee's name, rate, and hours worked and compute the resulting pay. Since this employee works different hours at different jobs, we are to do this for each day of the week. That is, compute the person's pay for Monday, Tuesday, Wednesday, and so on.

We could write a program that uses a FOR loop like the one below.

```
FOR INDEX: = 1 TO 5 DO
        BEGIN
                compute his pay after reading data
        END;
```

The only problem with this program is that it does not make clear just what we are doing (or trying to do!).

Suppose that we could write the program like this instead:

```
FOR DAY := MONDAY TO FRIDAY DO
      BEGIN
            compute pay after reading data
      END;
```

We might find this program segment somewhat easier to read. The only problem is that we must assure ourselves that the computer knows what MONDAY and FRIDAY really mean, and we must also be sure that the computer knows that TUESDAY follows MONDAY and so on. This is a pretty tall order for a dumb machine.

To make a long story short, it is possible to convey this information to the machine by defining our own type. The program fragments below illustrate this principle.

```
PROGRAM DEMO (OUTPUT);
   .
TYPE WEEKDAYS = (MONDAY, TUESDAY, WEDNESDAY,
                       THURSDAY, FRIDAY);
   .
VAR DAY : WEEKDAYS;
   .
BEGIN (* main *)
   .
FOR DAY : = MONDAY TO FRIDAY DO . . .
```

And so forth. How about that?

Let us explore just exactly what is going on before we go any further. The line

```
TYPE WEEKDAYS = (MONDAY, TUESDAY, WEDNESDAY,
                       THURSDAY, FRIDAY)
```

is the key to understanding the program.

In this line, we have defined to the machine a *new* type, one that it didn't know about before. This new type is not ambiguous at all—if anyone gives us an object and asks us whether or not that object is of type WEEKDAYS, it is possible to have an exact answer. For instance, if the object in question is *May*, then it is not of type WEEKDAYS. However, if the object is *Wednesday*, we would declare that the object is indeed of type WEEKDAYS. The object Sunday would not be of type WEEKDAYS.

It was necessary to mention DAY in the variables section of the program because DAY takes on the values associated with type WEEKDAYS. Furthermore, the definition of WEEKDAYS makes it clear that TUESDAY follows MONDAY, and so on. (FOR . . . DO . . . needs to know that!)

DAY was defined to be of type WEEKDAYS. This means that DAY can take on *only* those values associated with the type WEEKDAYS. It would be impossible to assign DAY := SATURDAY for example, since SATURDAY does not belong to the type WEEKDAYS.

Consider a second example:

```
TYPE GIRLS = (JOAN, JANE, JILL);
     BOYS = (HANK, FRED, JOHN);
VAR BOYSNAME : BOYS;
    GIRLSNAME : GIRLS;
BEGIN
    BOYSNAME := HANK;          (* legal *)
    GIRLSNAME := JOAN;         (* legal *)
    BOYSNAME := JANE;             (* type clash *)
    GIRLSNAME := ANNE;             (* ANNE is not defined *)
END
```

The ability to define your own types is one of the most important features of Pascal. This feature enables us to make our programs readable and allows us to use meaningful variable names.

6.4   SCALAR TYPES

In this section we will elaborate on how to make type definitions and how to make use of the definitions once we have made them.

One of the most important concepts behind the notion of type is that of *uniqueness*. That is, no object may belong to more than one type. The number 2 belongs to one type, and the number 2.0 is of a different type. The object 2 does not belong to more than one type. We say that types *do not intersect*.

If we keep this notion in mind when we define our own types, we will be able to avoid several pitfalls. Suppose for a moment that we were to define

```
TYPE DAYSOFWEEK = (MONDAY,TUESDAY,WEDNESDAY,
                   THURSDAY,FRIDAY,SATURDAY,
                   SUNDAY);
     WEEKEND = (SATURDAY,SUNDAY);
```

we then present the computer with the object SUNDAY and ask it to determine which type SUNDAY belongs to. Since SUNDAY appears in two definitions, it is not clear to which type it should belong, and the machine will protest. This is an error on the part of the programmer, who did not take care to make the type definitions *unique*. The definitions were allowed to intersect. The objects SATURDAY and SUNDAY were common to both definitions, and this overlap caused the machine to abort the program.

If we were to make a slight modification, like this:

TYPE DAYSOFWEEK = (MONDAY,TUESDAY,WEDNESDAY,
                   THURSDAY,FRIDAY);
     WEEKEND = (SATURDAY,SUNDAY);

the machine would not protest, since the definitions no longer intersect.

All of this discussion leads us to the notion of *scalar type*.[1]

We have already used scalar types in the section above. They are defined by specifying their members. We defined the scalar type WEEKEND by simply listing its members (SATURDAY,SUNDAY). These members were enclosed in parentheses as part of the requirements of Pascal.

If we want to define a type HOLIDAY, we can do so by simply listing its members. We might write

TYPE HOLIDAYS = (CHRISTMAS,EASTER,PASSOVER,
                 HANUKKAH);

or any other list that we desired.

By writing this list, we have done two things. First, we have defined the objects that belong to the type HOLIDAYS. Given any object, it is possible to determine whether or not it belongs to the type HOLIDAYS.

The second thing we have accomplished is less obvious. We have defined an *ordering* of the members of HOLIDAYS. We have, by the order in which we have written the list, declared to the machine that CHRISTMAS comes before EASTER, and EASTER comes before PASSOVER. This ordering was given to the machine by the programmer, who is solely responsible for it. If the programmer finds that HANUKKAH really comes before EASTER, he or she can simply change the ordering by writing the members of HOLIDAYS in a different order.

It was this feature that allowed us to write (in the example program of Section 6.3)

FOR DAY := MONDAY TO FRIDAY DO . . .

since the definition specified that MONDAY came before FRIDAY, and that there were objects in between.

Pascal has two special, built-in functions designed to deal with scalar types. These two functions are PRED and SUCC, which stand for "predecessor" and "successor" respectively. To illustrate their use, consider the following type:

TYPE MONTHS = (JAN,FEB,MAR,APR,MAY,JUN,JUL,AUG,SEP,
               OCT,NOV,DEC);

For this scalar type, the PRED(APR) is MAR, and the SUCC(JUN) is JUL.

---

[1]Scalar types are referred to as *enumerated types* in some books.

That is, PRED gives the member of the type that comes before, and SUCC gives the member of the type that comes after, the object that is named.

We see that SUCC(AUG) is SEP, and PRED(DEC) is NOV. Take care to realize, however, that PRED(JAN) does not exist! Similarly, SUCC(DEC) does not exist either. Moreover, there is no way to make a type "wrap around" into a circle as we might prefer. That is to say, each scalar type has only one single first element and one single last element.

How can we use the functions PRED and SUCC? Consider the following short segment of a Pascal program.

```
OLDMONTH := JAN;
WHILE OLDMONTH < DEC DO
    BEGIN
        IF OLDMONTH = JUN THEN OLDMONTH :=
                            SUCC (OLDMONTH)
    ELSE
            BEGIN
                Do a procedure to compute a payroll
                OLDMONTH := SUCC(OLDMONTH);
            END;
    END;
```

This code does not process the JUN payroll.

There is one "booby trap" which we will encounter when using scalar types. We really wish the following code would work:

```
FOR OLDMONTH := JAN TO DEC DO WRITELN (OLDMONTH);
```

but it won't!

The trouble lies not with the FOR loop—which does as we hoped it would and steps through the months of the year—but with the WRITELN procedure. The problem is a subtle one. OLDMONTH is a variable of type MONTH. MONTH is a type that contains certain symbols, namely the collection of letters JAN, FEB, and so on. These letters are the members of the scalar type MONTHS. They are not (alas) INTEGERS, or CHARs, or REALs, or even BOOLEANs, which are the only things that WRITELN has the ability to deal with. All we will get for our pains in the above line of code is a nasty error message. All is not lost, of course. With a little more work, we can achieve what we want. Try this:

```
FOR OLDMONTH := JAN TO DEC DO
    CASE OLDMONTH OF
        JAN : WRITELN ('January');
        FEB : WRITELN ('February');
              ⋮
        DEC : WRITELN ('December')
    END;
```

This code accomplishes the intended task, but with a little less panache.

6.5   SUBRANGE TYPES

Suppose that we are concerned with rainfall for the years 1881 to 1977. We desire that anyone asking about the rainfall for some other year be confronted with an error message, since we want to be sure that no mistake is made when running the program. If we want to restrict the membership of a new scalar type to include only certain members of an older, previously defined type, we can use a *subrange* type.

Suppose that we had declared

> TYPE MONTHS = (JAN,FEB,MAR,APR,MAY,JUN,JUL,AUG,SEP,
>   OCT,NOV,DEC);
>   SUMMER = JUN..AUG;

These type declarations make SUMMER a *subrange* of MONTHS. There is no conflict of membership between the types, since SUMMER is actually only a smaller part of MONTHS. When we wrote SUMMER = JUN..AUG, we were making use of JUN and AUG from the previous line, where the machine first learned about them. The two dots in type SUMMER say that everything between JUN and AUG is also included in the subrange type, so that JUL is also a member of type SUMMER.

In general, the use of subranges is a good idea. Suppose that the programmer is only interested in the years from 1881 to 1977 as part of a project. He could declare

> TYPE YEARS = 1881..1977;

Now if a variable of type YEARS were to happen to acquire (erroneously) some value other than integers between 1881 and 1977, say 1776, an error message would result. (*The message usually says something like RANGE ERROR.*)

Watch out for a common mistake—there are no parentheses around a subrange type definition.

6.6   OTHER TYPES

This chapter has presented us with one of our first real opportunities to expand upon the notion of type. If we reflect a moment, it may occur to us that the process of using basic types to define other types can be continued almost indefinitely; old types can be used to define newer types and subranges.

The meat of this concept is that definitions can be built one upon the other until we are able to build very useful objects with ease. Further discussion of this idea must be deferred until we have an opportunity to discuss RECORD types in Chapter 8 but rest assured that your instincts are sound.

There are still other types to be found in Pascal. One of the most useful of these is the SET. Entire college courses are taught about the concept of sets, and we will touch on the subject only briefly here.

Did you ever want to "idiot proof" a piece of code? Consider the following code segment:

```
WRITELN ('Give me a number between 1 and 7');
READLN (NUMBER);
CASE NUMBER OF
      1:something
      2:something else
         ⋮
      7:the last something
END;
```

If someone replies to the READLN with the number 8, your carefully constructed code will "blow up," and the CASE statement will not have a match.

A slight change, however, can "idiot proof" the code (although unfortunately it cannot do the same for the programmer!).

Consider:

```
REPEAT
      WRITELN ('Give me a number between one and seven');
      READLN (NUMBER)
UNTIL NUMBER IN [1,2,3,4,5,6,7]
CASE NUMBER OF
      ⋮
```

and so on. Now, the REPEAT . . . UNTIL . . . loop will cause the user of the program to have to enter numbers until he or she enters one correctly. Note the use of brackets rather than parentheses in line four. This signals the use of SET notation. The word IN shows that NUMBER is a member of the SET.

There are many uses for sets, but just this sort of program protection is one of their major applications. The concept of sets is covered in most intermediate textbooks on Pascal. If you happen to be familiar with set notation, you may use the following:

[   ]   (brackets) define the members of a set. Empty brackets show an empty set.

+   causes the union of two sets

*   shows set intersection

<=   is the subset symbol

>=   is the superset symbol

IN   determines set membership, like the epsilon of usual mathematics

The type declarations for sets are illustrated by:

TYPE POSITIVE = 1..10;
VAR ZPLUS : SET OF POSITIVE;

This would allow ZPLUS to be a set which can have any or all of the integers from 1 to 10 as its members.

6.7   EXAMPLES AND EXERCISES

Example 1

Define an appropriate scalar type for the colors of the flag.

Answer

TYPE COLOR = (RED,WHITE,BLUE);

Example 2

Write a program segment to take advantage of the scalar type from Example 1, to determine the cost of bunting for making flags.

Answer

TYPE COLOR = (RED,WHITE,BLUE);
VAR BUNTING : COLOR;
BEGIN
        FOR BUNTING := RED TO BLUE DO
                determine the cost;
END;

Example 3

Write a subrange definition to consist of parts of a larger type.

Answer

TYPE DESSERTS = (CAKE,CANDY,PIE,FRUIT,NUTS);
        PASTRIES = CAKE,PIE;
        (*or perhaps*)
        AFTERDINNER = CAKE..FRUIT;

Exercises

1.   Write a program which will allow you to input the hours a person works but which will blow up if the input is more than 60 hours or less than 0 hours. Use a subrange type of

TYPE LEGALHOURS = 0..60;

You should compile and run this program, since the use of subranges can cause confusion that should clear up with a little practice.

2. Inspect all of your previous program. (You *did* save them, didn't you?) See how the programs could benefit from using subrange types instead of the usual predefined type of INTEGER.

3. Write a code segment that allows a "menu" to be presented to a user of the program. This menu should consist of a list of several letters, from which the user is asked to input one. If the user does not use one of the legal letters, the program, instead of "bombing" should make the user try again. *Hint:* Use sets.

7.0

Arrays

7.1   THE NEED FOR ARRAYS

Up to now, we have been using Pascal to write programs which—while they may have been fun—have had little practical value. We need additional ability to allow us to manipulate data stored in the machine in a more elegant and efficient fashion. At the moment, some very simple programming assignments are beyond our ability. For instance, suppose someone wanted to read us a list of numbers in increasing order—that is, the smallest first, the next-smallest next, and so on. Suppose, further, that we were required to repeat back the numbers in *reverse* order. That is, we were to list the same numbers, only in decreasing order, from largest to smallest.

With our present capabilities, we cannot write (without undue tedium) a program to accomplish this task. What we need is the ability to make the machine retain *all* of the numbers that are given it, say in a sort of list, and then print the list from bottom to top.

This chapter is devoted to the definition and maintenance of such lists. They are usually referred to by the name *array*, but the concept remains the same. All we want to do is save a mass of data in some manner so that we can use it all at once. In other words, we want to be able to "see" all the data so that we can use or change any part of them.

Arrays give us the power to make the machine a useful tool and not just a toy. After you understand arrays, you will be able to make the machine a workhorse.

7.2   THE CONCEPT OF ARRAYS

Suppose that we were to present you with a set of boxes numbered from 1 to 10. If you were then given cards with the names of 10 people written on them, one to a card, and told to put the cards in the boxes, one to a box, you could do so. See the figure on the next page.

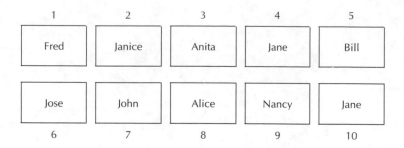

Now if someone asked you to write the name on the card which is in the fourth box, you could do it. In this case, you would write JANE. As a shorthand notation, we could refer to the fourth box as BOX[4]. Then BOX[5] above contains BILL.

The following code would make a list of the contents of all the boxes.

FOR I := 1 TO 10 DO WRITELN(BOX[I]);

This code would produce a list of the *contents* of all of the boxes. If we were to write

FOR I := 10 DOWNTO 1 DO WRITELN (BOX[I]);

we would get a list of the contents of the boxes *starting with the last box and moving to the first.*

In each of these code segments, we are using I as an "index." That is, I tells us where in the collection of boxes to look for something.

If we wanted to replace the contents of the fourth box with something else that we typed at the keyboard, we could write

READLN(BOX[4]);

If we desired to cause the contents of box 1 to be changed to have the same contents as box 7, we could write

BOX[1] := BOX[7];

7.3   USING ARRAYS

A set of "boxes" arranged in this fashion is called an *array*. Arrays provide us with a great deal of power. Like any other Pascal variable, they must be declared in the VAR section of the program. As an example, suppose that we wanted to create a set of eight boxes (we will soon start referring to them as *cells*, not boxes), each containing an integer. (We *have* to know what TYPE the contents will be.) Suppose our collection of boxes (cells) is to be known by the name of COSTS. Then we would have the following declaration in the VAR section of the program:

COSTS : ARRAY [1..8] OF INTEGER;

We note several things about this declaration. The [1..8] tells the machine to reserve eight cells, numbered from 1 through 8, for the contents of the array. The array is called COSTS, and it contains integers. Note that we did not write INTEGERS, but only INTEGER. Like other Pascal statements, this one is followed by a semicolon.

Note further that this statement only creates the cells; it does NOT put anything in them! If we want the contents to be certain things, we must put the contents in the array ourselves. For instance, the code

FOR INDEX := 1 TO 8 DO COSTS[INDEX] := 97;

would load each of the cells with the integer 97. By the way, we would have to be sure that INDEX was a variable of type INTEGER, since the numbers 1 through 8 are integers. This does not have anything to do with the contents of the cells also being integers.

As an example problem, suppose that someone asks us to listen to a list of 10 letters, and then repeat them back in the reverse order from that in which we heard them. That is, the last letter we heard should be repeated back first, and so on, until we finally come to the first letter that we heard. The following program will accomplish this task.

```
PROGRAM DEMO (INPUT, OUTPUT);
    VAR INDEX: INTEGER;
        LETTERS: ARRAY[1..10] OF CHAR;
    BEGIN
        FOR INDEX:=1 TO 10 DO READLN (LETTERS[INDEX]);
        FOR INDEX:=10 DOWNTO 1 DO WRITELN
                    (LETTERS[INDEX]);
    END.
```

The first FOR loop loads the contents (the letters) into the array, and the second loop prints the contents out.

Arrays can be made to contain any type of data that one wishes, including user-defined types. See if you can sort out what the following code does.

```
PROGRAM DEMO1 (INPUT, OUTPUT);
    TYPE DAY = (SUN, MON, TUE, WED, THU, FRI, SAT);
        WORKTHATDAY = (YES,NO);
    VAR LIST : ARRAY [DAY] OF WORKTHATDAY;
        INDEX : DAY;
    BEGIN
        FOR INDEX := MON TO FRI DO LIST[INDEX] := YES;
        LIST[SAT] := NO; LIST[SUN] := NO;
    END.
```

This code makes a set of seven boxes, each labeled with a day of the week, and puts either a yes or a no in the box corresponding to a particular day.

As yet another example, if one wished to have a set of boxes labeled with years in order to keep a record of total rainfall for a period of time (say from 1881 to 1980) we could do this:

VAR RAINFALL: ARRAY [1881..1980] OF REAL:

and then

FOR INDEX : = 1881 TO 1980 DO WRITELN (RAINFALL[INDEX]);

would write out the rainfall for each year (provided we had previously read it in!).

Arrays give us a lot of power. They provide quick access to the contents of many different storage positions, and they work with the contents of particular parts of data sets while ignoring other parts. They do have some drawbacks, however.

One is that we must know how big to make an array to begin with. That is, we must know how many cells to create in the VAR section of the program before we even start. In some situations this can be a major problem. Suppose someone told you to add the contents of 100 cells of an array called LIST.[1] You could do so with the following code:

SUM : = 0.0;
FOR INDEX : = 1 TO 100 DO SUM : = SUM + LIST[INDEX];

However, if someone were to ask you to write a program that would sum the grades on a test for the class, you would have to first know how many tests there were in order to create the array to hold the grades. You are faced with either taking a guess (and maybe being wrong) or counting the grades before you begin. The usual practice is to take an educated but conservative guess.

7.4   MAKING ARRAY TYPES

Having convinced ourselves that arrays may be useful tools to have around, we now proceed to see just how to set up a program so it can use them.

Suppose I want to arrange an array to hold the rainfall data for the last 100 years. In RAIN[1891] (for instance), I would like to find 17.15, indicating that in the year 1891 there were 17.15 inches of rainfall. I could then do this:

VAR RAIN : ARRAY [1880..1980] OF REAL;

Now RAIN is an array, with 101 (count them!) boxes, each of which can hold a real number. If we were to ask for the rainfall for the year 1981, we would WRITELN (RAIN[1981]); and be rewarded with an error mes-

---

[1]We assume that LIST contains REAL or INTEGER numbers.

sage, because we have not arranged for a "box" for the year 1981. However, we could store the rainfall for any year between 1880 and 1980 with no trouble.

The items that go between the brackets are what tell the machine how much space to reserve for the array. Arrays can be indexed by any scalar type or scalar subrange type. For instance, suppose that we define the scalar type DAYOFWEEK by

TYPE DAYOFWEEK = (MON,TUES,WEDS,THURS,FRI);

Then we could make a set of boxes—i.e., an array indexed by the days of the week—in this way:

VAR DAYS : ARRAY [DAYOFWEEK] OF REAL;

or (equivalently)

VAR DAYS: ARRAY[MON..FRI] OF REAL;

A more complex application is to make arrays with more than one dimension. That is we can arrange the boxes both in rows and columns, and even more. Suppose that we do the following:

TYPE ROWS = 1..20;
     COLUMNS = 1..40;

VAR BOXES : ARRAY [ROWS,COLUMNS] OF REAL;

Then BOXES is an array with 20 rows and 40 columns. That is, BOXES has 800 "slots" for data (20 × 40).

This approach could be very useful if I wanted to store say, the grades on each of 10 tests for a class of 30 students. I could do this:

TYPE STUDENTS = 1..30;
     TESTS = 1..10;

VAR GRADES: ARRAY [STUDENTS,TESTS] OF REAL;

Now GRADES[4,9], for instance, would contain the ninth grade of the fourth student.

7.5   EXAMPLES AND EXERCISES

There are several exercises and examples in this section. It will be a big help to you if you work your way through them all.

The first example is rather a difficult one, but it illustrates several points.

Example 1

Write a program to count the number of occurrences of each letter of the alphabet in a given line of text.

Answer

```
PROGRAM COUNT (INPUT,OUTPUT);
TYPE ALPHABET = 'A'..'Z'; (* this is a scalar type *)
VAR COUNTS : ARRAY [ALPHABET] OF INTEGER;
     LETTER : ALPHABET;
BEGIN
     (* load COUNTS with all zeroes before you get any letters *)
     FOR LETTER := 'A' TO 'Z' DO COUNTS[LETTER] := 0;
     (* the main logic *)
     READ (LETTER);
          (* read the first letter *)
     WHILE NOT EOLN DO
        BEGIN
             COUNTS[LETTER] := COUNTS[LETTER] + 1;
             READ (LETTER);
          END;
     (* this adds one to the particular box that carries the label of
     the particular letter that was read *)
     (* the function EOLN is built into Pascal and detects the End Of
     a LiNe *)
     (* now we will write out the counts for each letter of the alpha-
     bet *)
     FOR LETTER := 'A' TO 'Z' DO
             WRITELN (COUNTS[LETTER]);
END.
```

Here are some questions concerning this example:

1. How could the program be modified to count lowercase letters as
    well?

2. Can the program be made to deal with punctuation?
    Hint: Modify the TYPE

3. Fix the program so that a blank does not make it "blow up."
    Hint: Try ALPHABET = ' '..'Z';

4. As a crowning touch, try
    COUNTS : ARRAY[CHAR] OF INTEGER;
    and use things like

    FOR LETTER := CHR(0) TO CHR(255) DO . . .

   If you want to know what CHR does, you have the ability to write a
short program to find out!

Exercises

1. Read 10 numbers from the keyboard, and write them back out in the reverse order from the way you read them. (Use an array to hold the numbers as they come in, and make use of FOR...DO... loops.)

2. There are 20 students in a class, and each has taken 10 tests. Write a program to
    a.   Read 10 scores for each student into the machine.
    b.   Compute and print each student's average.
    c.   Compute and print the class average for each test.
    d.   Compute and print the overall class average.

    Hint:

    ```
    FOR I := 1 TO NBROFSTUDENTS DO
        FOR J := 1 TO NBROFGRADES DO
            .

            .
            ....GRADE[I,J]...
            .

            .
    ```

A comment on some techniques: For several of the following exercises, we need to be able to "find the largest one" or pick from an entire array a particular cell that meets a certain requirement. Consider the following code segment:

```
J := 1;
FOR I := 1 TO NBROFCELLS DO
            IF MATRIX[I] > MATRIX[J] THEN J := I;
WRITELN ('The largest element is in cell number ',J);
WRITELN ('The largest element is ', MATRIX[J]);
```

This code segment finds the largest element in an array. Now consider the following code:

```
J := 0;
FOR I := 1 TO NBROFCELLS DO
            IF MATRIX[I] = 17 THEN J := I; (* see note below *)
If J = 0 THEN WRITELN ('17 is not in the array')
ELSE WRITELN ('17 is in the array and is in cell number ', J);
```

This code segment finds a particular cell in the array. In this case, it finds the cell that contains a 17. If no 17 is found, it tells us that as well. (*Note:* The FOR...DO... loop in this example continues searching through the array even after a 17 is found. It could be rewritten as a WHILE...DO... to avoid unnecessary searching.)

3. I will have an array that records the rainfall for the years 1881 to 1977. I want to write the average rainfall for these 97 years, the year in which the most rain occurred, and the year of least rainfall. Write a program to do all this. (Figure 7–1 will provide you with information if you want it.)

Figure 7–1

Year	Rain	Year	Rain
1881	16. 16	1930	17. 58
1882	24. 76	1931	18. 35
1883	28. 21	1932	21. 14
1884	33. 91	1933	12. 22
1885	37. 07	1934	13. 33
1886	23. 05	1935	15. 49
1887	22. 83	1936	19. 72
1888	16. 51	1937	17. 10
1889	19. 40	1938	19. 10
1890	15. 41	1939	21. 01
1891	17. 15	1940	13. 62
1892	15. 60	1941	37. 21
1893	17. 23	1942	21. 62
1894	15. 81	1943	18. 38
1895	24. 79	1944	23. 60
1896	24. 28	1945	17. 19
1897	19. 16	1946	20. 80
1898	22. 54	1947	15. 48
1899	27. 39	1948	24. 38
1900	24. 40	1949	25. 15
1901	24. 42	1950	23. 18
1902	23. 11	1951	25. 29
1903	20. 28	1952	12. 15
1904	21. 33	1953	13. 05
1905	32. 31	1954	13. 89
1906	24. 92	1955	13. 71
1907	18. 09	1956	9. 94
1908	19. 05	1957	21. 24
1909	19. 52	1958	23. 29
1910	11. 15	1959	22. 81
1911	22. 73	1960	36. 67
1912	15. 08	1961	22. 44
1913	18. 97	1962	29. 76
1914	19. 27	1963	17. 30
1915	27. 65	1964	17. 97
1916	16. 43	1965	20. 09
1917	17. 06	1966	14. 91
1918	18. 12	1967	16. 85
1919	22. 01	1968	17. 97
1920	21. 82	1969	22. 55
1921	25. 24	1970	9. 56
1922	19. 85	1971	23. 04
1923	39. 75	1972	15. 34
1924	17. 90	1973	18. 05
1925	23. 53	1974	23. 09
1926	26. 25	1975	21. 08
1927	15. 42	1976	16. 24
1928	32. 34	1977	20. 18
1929	18. 87		

The information in this figure is reproduced with the kind permission of the *Amarillo Daily News*.

4. We want to read a date of the form MM/DD/YY and print it in the form

MONTH DAY,YEAR.

Write a program to do this. This program could later be used as a procedure in other programs. *Hint:*

```
VAR MONTH : ARRAY [1..12] OF STRING;
BEGIN
      MONTH[1] := 'January'; MONTH[2] := 'February'; etc.

      CASE MM OF ...
```

Important note: This program depends on having available UCSD Pascal or some other implementation which uses type STRING.

5. A utility company has five different rates that it charges customers, depending upon that customer's temperament and employment. Write a program that will read a basic bill and apply one of the five factors to that bill. The program should ask for the basic amount and the rate number, and produce the amount owed. Use the following rate factors:

    1   1.99
    2   1.50
    3   1.25
    4   1.125
    5   1.0

    A line in your program might be

```
BILL := BASICAMOUNT * RATE[I];
```

8.0

Chapter 8

Dynamic data structures

8.1   INTRODUCTION

In using arrays, we discovered only one major drawback: it was necessary to know how big to make the array when we wrote the program. Once the number of cells in the array had been specified (in the VAR section), we could not change it without also changing the program and recompiling it. For this reason, arrays are known in Pascal as *static* data structures. That is, once specified, their size cannot be changed.

In this chapter, we will meet some of the *dynamic* data structures. We can change the size or even the shape of these structures to meet the current requirements of the program.

If a programmer using a particular array suddenly needed more cells than were originally specified, he or she would have to rewrite the program and then recompile it. By using the dynamic structures, we can change the size of structures *at run time* without penalty and without recompiling or otherwise changing the program.

This feature distinguishes Pascal from many of the other common computer languages, such as FORTRAN.

Dynamic data structures are such powerful tools that learning how to tame and handle them will be well worth your time. That is the objective of this chapter.

8.2   PROBLEMS THAT NEED DYNAMIC DATA STRUCTURES

Dynamic data structures comprise one of the most powerful features of Pascal. We will begin by pointing out a couple of situations, represented by the arrays in Figures 8–1 and 8–2.

Suppose that someone asks us to add the number 7 between the 6 and the 8 in Figure 8–1. In order to do that, we must first move the 8 and all the elements below it down one cell and then insert the 7 in the cell which

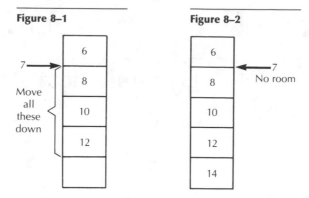

Figure 8–1   **Figure 8–2**

used to contain the 8. This represents a lot of data movement, which takes quite a bit of computer time. (What if the array were 10,000 cells long instead of only 5?)

An even worse case is represented by Figure 8–2, where there is just no room in the array for the additional element. We cannot create an additional cell since the array, once created, cannot change size.

The answer lies in creating a different kind of data structure (see Figure 8–3).

We refer to the arrows in Figure 8–3 as *pointers*. By starting with the 6 and following the pointers, we can go through the entire list, just as we could go through the entire array of Figure 8–2. The pointer from the last cell (14) is "grounded" to show that this *is* the last cell and that its pointer points nowhere.

Ignoring for a moment the problems of How do we set this up? let's tackle the problem of What can we do with it? Suppose someone tells us to add a 7 between the 6 and the 8. This time, we will create a new place just for the 7 and adjust the pointers to indicate that the 7 now lies between the 6 and the 8. Figure 8–4 illustrates this process; the dotted line represents an old arrow, from Figure 8–3, and the solid lines represent the new arrows that we put in.

In order to create Figure 8–4 from Figure 8–3, *all* that we have to do is "invent" the 7, make the arrow from the 6 point to the 7, and draw a new arrow from the 7 to the 8. The rest of the numbers remain completely undisturbed. We don't have to move any of the numbers, but just change

Figure 8–3

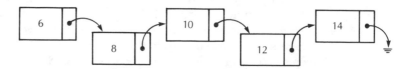

Figure 8–4

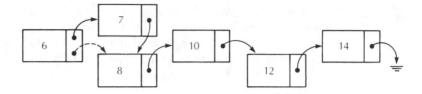

a few arrows. This approach results in considerable savings of computer time, and in addition it solves several problems which were illustrated in Figures 8–1 and 8–2. All we have to do is learn how to work the "magic."

8.3 RECORDS AND POINTERS

There are two built-in Pascal data types that will help us with our present task. They are RECORD and POINTER. As we might guess, POINTER is a type that lets us represent the arrows shown in Figure 8–4 in a convenient fashion.

Referring to Figure 8–4 again, we see that each member of the list really has two parts: the actual data and the pointer to the next member of the list. That is, we have to provide two items for each member of the list. Pascal includes a convenient method for doing this.

Let us digress for a moment and consider a slightly different problem. Suppose that we want to have a list of persons, each with a name, address, and zip code. Pascal allows us to group items that "go together" by use of the RECORD type.

Consider:

```
TYPE PERSON = RECORD
                NAME, ADDRESS, ZIP : STRING;
              END;
(* We must have previously defined the type STRING *)
VAR JIM, JOHN, JACK : PERSON;
```

Now, if we want to refer to the address of Jim, we could say WRITELN (JIM.ADDRESS);. Notice the "dot" between JIM and ADDRESS. If we wanted the zip code for Jack, we would say WRITELN (JACK.ZIP);. It is clear that if the portion of memory containing Jim's record needed to move to another part of the machine, we would have to move *all* of the record and not just the name.

For the present discussion, we can regard RECORD as a means of grouping several items together in the machine. In particular, we will utilize this as a method for making data and an associated pointer travel together for the problems of Figures 8–3 and 8–4.

Now we can deal with the problem of producing a Pascal program to accomplish the task that we represented in Figures 8–3 and 8–4 above. That is, we will arrange a program so that we have the power to create lists that have elements with two parts, one of which is the data, the other a pointer. Examine the following program:

```
TYPE PTR =  ↑NODE;
       NODE = RECORD
                      DATA : INTEGER;
                      LINK : PTR;
              END;
       VAR P,Q : PTR;
```

We have a lot to discuss! First, the little arrow (↑) means that type PTR is a *pointer* to something called NODE. In the variables section, we see that P and Q are pointers to nodes (whatever *they* are).

The NODEs themselves consist of two parts which travel together. These two parts are (in this case) a piece of data of type INTEGER and a link which is a pointer to another node (since that is what type PTR means).

Now consider Figure 8–5.

We want to create a new node which will contain a 7 as data, which will be pointed to by the link of the node containing 6, and whose link will point to the node containing 8.

For convenience, we will let P (remember that P is a variable of type PTR) be a pointer to the node which contains the 6 as data.

Some discussion of notation is in order. The placement of the little arrow can be quite confusing. When the arrow is on the *left* of something, as in TYPE PTR = ↑NODE, above, it means that PTR is a pointer *to* a node. If we write instead, P↑, with the arrow on the right, it means "the thing that is pointed to by P."

In Figure 8–5, P↑.DATA is 6, and P↑.LINK points to the node which contains the 8 as data. That is, P↑.LINK↑.DATA is 8. Wow!

We now tackle the problem of adding a 7 between the 6 and the 8. We first need to create a new node that will contain 7 as its data. We do this in Pascal as follows:

Figure 8–5

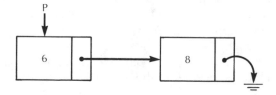

NEW(Q);   (* remember that Q is of type PTR, and hence Q points to nodes, so that this statement makes a new node, and makes Q point to it *)

Q↑.DATA := 7;   (* sets the data field of the new node to 7 *)

Now we need to "hook it in" by adjusting the pointers. The LINK field of the new node should point where the link field of the 6 now points, so we write

Q↑.LINK := P↑.LINK;

Also, the link field of the 6 should point to the new node, Q, so we write P↑.LINK := Q;.

This means that it took four statements to insert the 7 between the 6 and the 8. Not too bad.

A word of caution: Study this example—it is an important one. Figure 8–6 shows graphically the effect of each of the four statements discussed above.

8.4   NEW and DISPOSE

In the section preceding this one we used the built-in Pascal procedure NEW to "create something out of nothing." It was used to reserve space in the machine for a new node and also to cause a pointer to point to that new node. We did this by saying NEW(Q), which "invented" storage space for a node and arranged for Q to point to that storage space. Since this was accomplished "on the fly" by the program, we call this an example of "dynamic allocation." That is, our program needed a new storage location in the middle of its execution; so it "invented" one.

If we were to continue to invent new nodes, eventually we would use up all the memory of the machine, since newly created nodes do not overlap or destroy old ones. It makes sense that, if we were to tell the machine to destroy, or "deallocate," nodes which are no longer useful to us, we could then create new nodes that would use the same storage locations that the old ones did. This procedure would let us reuse the memory and thus allow us to store more.

Suppose that Q is a pointer to a node and that we are no longer in need of that node or its contents. We can tell the machine to destroy that node by saying DISPOSE(Q). This tells the machine that the contents of the node pointed to by Q are no longer needed, and so the memory locations that hold those contents can be reused. Of course the contents are destroyed when we tell the machine to DISPOSE(Q). After that operation, Q no longer points anywhere.

For various reasons, on some machines DISPOSE does not work properly. NEW works in all machines that run Pascal, to the knowledge of this author.

Figure 8–6

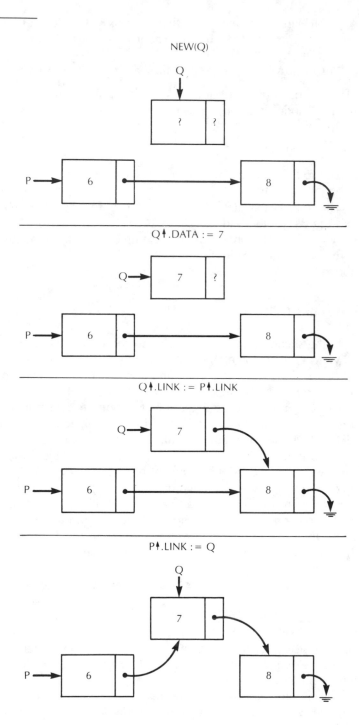

NEW(Q)

Q↑.DATA := 7

Q↑.LINK := P↑.LINK

P↑.LINK := Q

8.5   EXAMPLES AND EXERCISES

Exercises

1.   This exercise is concerned only with record structures. Given:

```
TYPE PERSON = RECORD
                    IDNO : INTEGER;
                    PAY : REAL;
              END;
VAR PAYROLL : ARRAY [1..100] OF PERSON;
     •
     •
```

Write a program that will print the IDNO of each employee who makes more than $5,200. *Hint:*

```
FOR I := 1 TO 100 DO
     IF (PAYROLL[I].PAY > 5200.00) THEN WRITELN
     (PAYROLL[I].IDNO);
```

Your main job is to figure out how to read the data into the machine in the first place. *Additional hint:*

```
READLN (PAYROLL[I].IDNO,PAYROLL[I].PAY);
```

2.   To find out whether DISPOSE works properly on your machine, run the following program. If it works, then so does DISPOSE. If the program gives some type of error message indicating that the machine is out of memory, then DISPOSE does not work on your machine.

```
PROGRAM TEST(OUTPUT);
     TYPE PTR =  ↑NODE;
          NODE = RECORD
                       JUNK: ARRAY[1..500] OF CHAR;
                       LINK : PTR;
                  END;
     VAR Q: PTR;
         INDEX: INTEGER;
     BEGIN
          FOR INDEX := 1 TO 10000 DO
               BEGIN
                    NEW(Q);
                    DISPOSE(Q);
               END;
          WRITELN ('DISPOSE works');
     END.
```

This program does its job by creating a lot of nodes of large size and then attempting to use DISPOSE to destroy them. If DISPOSE works properly, then each node will be destroyed immediately after its creation, and the machine will complete the program. If DISPOSE doesn't work properly, the nodes will not be destroyed and will quickly fill the available memory, causing the program to "crash."

3. A queue is a waiting line; people arrive at the end of the line and depart from the front. We rule out other possibilities, such as "butting in." A nice example is a line of people waiting to get to a bank teller. We can represent a queue by a *linked list* as shown below.

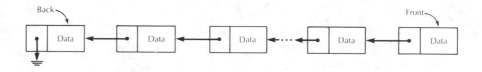

The arrows are pointers, and the boxes are records. Specifically, use:

```
TYPE PTR = ↑ NODE;
        NODE = RECORD
                        DATA : (*for example*) REAL;
                        LINK : PTR;
                END;
        VAR FRONT,BACK,Q : PTR;
```

The following examples illustrate how to use this code.

Example 1

Write a procedure that will list the data in the queue.

Answer

```
PROCEDURE LIST;
    BEGIN
            Q := FRONT;
            WHILE Q <> NIL DO (* NIL is the "ground" symbol for
                                        Pascal *)
                    BEGIN
                            WRITELN (Q ↑ .DATA);
                            Q := Q ↑ .LINK;
                    END;
    END;
```

Example 2

Write a procedure that will add a new node to the back of the queue.

Answer

```
PROCEDURE ADD;
    BEGIN
            NEW(Q);
            READLN (Q ↑ .DATA);
            Q ↑ .LINK : = NIL;
            BACK ↑ .LINK : = Q;
            BACK : = Q;
    END;
```

Exercise

4. Write a procedure that will remove the front node from the queue and still leave a queue. Expand this procedure to deal with the case of an empty queue.

Example 3

A "stack" is like a pile of pancakes; additions and deletions occur only at the top of the pile.

Using the same definitions of PTR and NODE as before, consider:

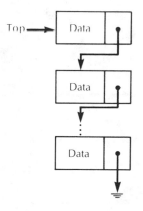

Using VAR Q,TOP : PTR; we can write a procedure LIST to list the contents of the stack. Note that this procedure is a lot like the list procedure for the queue.

```
PROCEDURE LIST;
    BEGIN
        Q := TOP;
        WHILE Q <> NIL DO
            BEGIN
                WRITELN (Q↑.DATA);
                Q := Q↑.LINK;
            END;
    END;
```

Exercise

5. Can you write procedures PUSH and POP to add nodes to the top of the stack and also delete them from the top?

9.0

Chapter 9

Recursion

9.1   INTRODUCTION

This chapter is devoted to yet another concept that sets Pascal apart from some other languages. Recursion actually is a phenomenon that we often meet in everyday life, but perhaps we haven't attached importance to it before.

Suppose that we have a television camera (perhaps on a home video recorder) and a television set that is hooked to the camera in such a way that whatever the camera "sees" is shown on the television screen. Now suppose that a man is standing by the television screen, and the camera is trained on both at the same time. What will then show up on the screen? What we would expect to see is a picture that contains a picture that contains a picture, and so on until the pictures get too small to be seen. What we do not expect (and wouldn't happen) is that the television set, the camera, or the man would blow up, burn out, or refuse to work.

We extend this analogy to computer programming, keeping in mind that there is no reason to expect explosions—in the computer, the program, or the programmer.

What we will find is that the concept of recursion can lead to some very elegant and simple, yet very powerful, programs.

9.2   WHAT IS RECURSION?

Recursion is a concept that will sometimes allow us to express some rather complicated programs in a very simple fashion. Simply stated, we say that a procedure (or a function) uses *recursion* (or is *recursive*) if that procedure calls itself as a procedure. This may sound a little "hairy" to FORTRAN or BASIC programmers, so let us explore the concept a bit.

Suppose that we have a procedure named A which calls a procedure named B. This situation is illustrated in Figure 9–1.

Figure 9–1

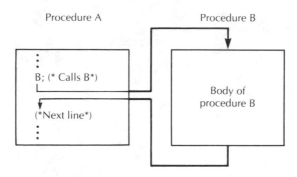

In this case, the program flow is as follows: The machine executes code from procedure A until it encounters the line in procedure A that directs the machine to "jump" to procedure B. After the machine has executed procedure B, it returns to procedure A. Specifically, the machine, after returning from procedure B, executes the statement *after* the statement that called procedure B.

Now, in your mind (because this isn't quite the way it really happens), suppose that procedure B is replaced by a carbon copy of procedure A. The result is a procedure that "calls itself." This process (that of calling itself) is known as *recursion*.

One might immediately ask the question, If the procedure calls itself, then how can it ever return at all? The answer lies in the way procedure A is actually coded. It usually contains a statement similar to IF . . . THEN A; which allows procedure A to call itself only if a condition is met. More on this later.

There are two kinds of recursion, and they are illustrated in Figure 9–2. In the first kind, called *direct* recursion, a procedure calls itself directly. In the second kind, called *indirect* recursion, the first procedure calls a second procedure (which is distinct), which may call other procedures, until finally one of them calls the first procedure again. By following the trail of called procedures, one discovers that the system is recursive.

9.3   AN EXAMPLE OF RECURSION

Recursion in any form is forbidden in FORTRAN, and this causes some very hard-to-find errors and unpredictable happenings. If a set of subroutines is ill-constructed, it is possible to include accidental indirect recursion, and this blows many FORTRAN systems to shreds.

Pascal does not have this kind of problem. In Pascal, not only is recur-

Figure 9–2

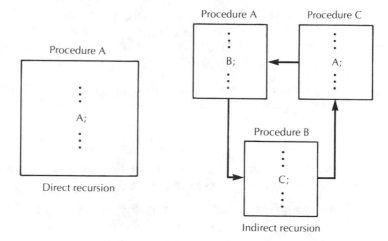

Procedure A

A;

Direct recursion

Procedure A

B;

Procedure C

A;

Procedure B

C;

Indirect recursion

sion legal, but it can be used to simplify considerably the programmer's task.

"Easy" examples of recursive programming are hard to come by. The real power of the technique lies in making some very complicated programming become simple. The problem is that one needs to understand the complicated program, too.

Suppose that we write a program segment to draw a line of a certain length, say of length X. The program segment

```
FOR I := 1 TO X DO WRITE ('*'); WRITELN;
```

will draw a "line" of asterisks of length X on the paper.

Now suppose that we wanted to start with a line, say, of length 100, then draw a second line of length 50, then draw a third line of length 25, and so forth until we draw a line of length 1. At that point we want to quit. We might accomplish this task in this fashion:

```
X := 100; (*be sure X is of type INTEGER*)
WHILE X > = 1 DO
     BEGIN
          FOR I := 1 TO X DO WRITE ('*'); WRITELN;
          X := X DIV 2;
     END;
```

Just for the sake of illustration, we could write:

```
PROCEDURE LINE (X : INTEGER);
     BEGIN
          IF X > = 1 THEN
```

```
                    BEGIN
                         FOR I := 1 TO X DO WRITE ('*'); WRITELN;
                         X := X DIV 2;
                         LINE (X);
                    END;
               END; (* of procedure LINE *)
```

This is probably the hard way to write the program, but the point is to illustrate recursion. By setting

```
     X := 100;
     LINE(X);
```

in the main program, we will write a number of lines of asterisks.

Suppose that we rearrange things slightly:

```
     PROCEDURE LINE (X : INTEGER);
          BEGIN
               IF X > = 1 THEN
                    BEGIN
                         X := X DIV 2;
                         LINE(X);
                         FOR I := 1 TO X DO WRITE ('*'); WRITELN;
                    END;
          END;
```

Now what do you suppose the following program segment will do?

```
     X := 100;
     LINE(X);
```

The best advice the author can give at this point is that the student load up these program segments and try them!

In order to understand just what is going on, we will discuss the following procedure:

```
   . PROCEDURE LINE (X : INTEGER);
          BEGIN
               IF X < = 1 THEN
                    BEGIN
                         FOR I := 1 TO X DO WRITE ('*'); WRITELN;
                         X := X DIV 2;
                         LINE(X);
                    END;
          END;
```

This procedure first draws a line of asterisks, then draws a line of asterisks which is only half as long. It continues this process until the length (X) of the line is less than 1, at which time the procedure is exited. Note that we are using the construction that has procedure LINE called by itself, but that the call is part of the THEN clause of an IF . . . THEN . . . statement. It is the IF statement that allows the procedure finally to halt.

The use of this procedure seems fairly straightforward, and it really presents no surprises. The surprise comes later, when we load the second version of procedure LINE, which has the FOR loop under the call to procedure LINE. For convenience, we rewrite it below:

```
PROCEDURE LINE (X : INTEGER);
    BEGIN
        IF X < = 1 THEN
            BEGIN
                X := X DIV 2;
                LINE(X);
                FOR I := 1 TO X DO WRITE ('*'); WRITELN;
            END;
    END;
```

This second example is a little harder to follow, but it illustrates how Pascal handles recursion.

Suppose that we start X at 100 and then call the procedure. Since X is greater than 1, the THEN clause is executed. X is divided by 2 and thus replaced by 50. The procedure LINE is then called again, with X equal to 50. Since the new X is still greater than 1, it is divided by 2 again, giving 25, and then procedure LINE is called again. This continues until X is less than 1. However, *each time LINE is called, Pascal saves the value of X.*

While the condition X < = 1 is false, LINE has been called *seven* times, and the machine has saved seven different values of X. Now when the program returns from the seventh call to LINE, it encounters the latest saved value of X, which is 1. (This is the seventh value of X which was saved.) Consequently, Pascal draws a line of one asterisk, and then returns to the sixth call to LINE, and to the sixth saved value of X, which is 3. The program prints 3 asterisks, and then returns to the fifth call, to the point where the saved value of X was 6, and prints 6 asterisks, and so on, until the last return from LINE prints 100 asterisks.

This is a pretty complicated system, but most of it is automatically taken care of by the Pascal compiler.

We comment that the combination

```
X := X DIV 2;
LINE(X);
```

could have been written

```
LINE(X DIV 2);
```

because we passed X by value.

Chapter 10 presents many problems on which you can exercise your programming skills. Among these are two that are especially appropriate for applying recursive techniques. These are the problems concerning the linked list and the binary tree (Problems 15 and 16).

The following procedure may be of use when you work on the binary tree program.

```
PROCEDURE ADD(P:PTR);
    BEGIN
        IF NEWDATA < = P↑.DATA THEN
            IF P↑.LEFT = NIL THEN
                P↑.LEFT := Q
            ELSE ADD(P↑.LEFT)
        ELSE
            IF P↑.RIGHT = NIL THEN
                P↑.RIGHT := Q
            ELSE ADD(P↑.RIGHT);
    END;
```

More details on recursion can be found in many fine books, including Lewis and Smith's *Applying Data Structures,* N. Wirth's *Algorithms + Data Structures = Programs,* from which we adapted the "television" example at the beginning of this chapter, the *Pascal User's Manual and Report* by K. Jensen and N. Wirth, or the forthcoming *Approaches to Data Structures* by B. Walker.

9.4   EXAMPLES AND EXERCISES

Example 1

Let us return for a moment to the concept of a linked list. Example 1 of Chapter 8 involved a procedure that would list the contents of a queue.

With recursion available to us, we can write a procedure that looks like this:

```
PROCEDURE LIST(P : PTR);
    BEGIN
        IF P <> NIL THEN
            BEGIN
                WRITELN (P↑.DATA);   (* these *)
                LIST(P↑.LINK);   (* these*)
            END;
    END;
```

In the main program we will have a line that says:

```
LIST(FRONT);
```

This will list the contents of the queue. It may not look like an improvement to the casual observer. May we suggest that you reverse the two statements marked with (* these *) and then run the program again?

After you realize just what has happened, you may want to attempt to write nonrecursive code to do the same thing. Such an exercise quickly convinces even the most skeptical that recursion has some merits!

Example 2

This exercise involves a classic puzzle known as the Towers of Hanoi. We will introduce it in several steps. First, draw three circles on a piece of paper. Now stack four coins—a penny, a nickel, a dime, and a quarter—on the leftmost circle, arranged from largest to smallest, with the largest coin on the bottom. That is, the stack of coins should have the quarter on the bottom, the nickel next, then the penny, and finally the dime. We have provided the circles below, but the reader will have to provide the coins!

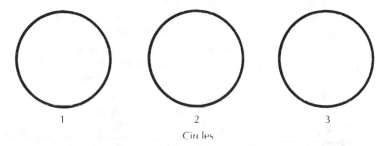

1   2   3

Circles

The objective is to move the stack of coins from the first (leftmost) circle to the third (rightmost) circle. Since this is a puzzle, there is of course a catch. There are two rules:

1. Coins must be moved one at a time.

2. A larger (in diameter) coin may never be stacked above a smaller coin.

After the reader has attempted this for a while, he or she may refer to the following set of directions to see that this task can be accomplished.

How to solve the puzzle

1. Move a coin from circle 1 to circle 2.

2. Move a coin from circle 1 to circle 3.

3. Move a coin from circle 2 to circle 3.

4.   Move a coin from circle 1 to circle 2.

5.   Move a coin from circle 3 to circle 1.

6.   Move a coin from circle 3 to circle 2.

7.   Move a coin from circle 1 to circle 2.

8.   Move a coin from circle 1 to circle 3.

9.   Move a coin from circle 2 to circle 3.

10.   Move a coin from circle 2 to circle 1.

11.   Move a coin from circle 3 to circle 1.

12.   Move a coin from circle 2 to circle 3.

13.   Move a coin from circle 1 to circle 2.

14.   Move a coin from circle 1 to circle 3.

15.   Move a coin from circle 2 to circle 3.

Legend has it that there are three "towers" located in Hanoi, with 64 golden disks of graduated size located on the first tower. A group of devoted religious men is dedicated to moving the 64 golden disks from the first tower to the third, following the rules of the game. When the task is accomplished, the world is supposed to come to an end. (Actually, we are pretty safe: it takes more than 1.8 times 10 to the *19th* moves, and if the disks weigh 50 pounds each, . . .)

For fewer than six or seven disks, it is not out of the question for us to write a program giving the directions for solving the puzzle. More than about seven disks will result in a *very* large set of instructions. A puzzle with five disks can be solved in 31 moves, a puzzle with six disks requires 63 moves, and a puzzle with seven disks requires 127 moves. (The number of moves is approximately doubled every time we add a disk. The actual number is 2 to the Nth, minus 1.)

If we had to write a program that did not use recursion to solve this problem, it might prove very difficult. We choose to attempt to develop a recursive solution.

Suppose that there are N disks located on the first tower when we start. In order to move the bottom disk at all, it is necessary for us to reach an intermediate stage where all of the disks but the last one are on the second tower, and the third tower is empty. We reached this stage after move number 7 in the four-coin problem. This intermediate stage *had* to occur, because otherwise there would be no way for the largest disk to be moved from the first tower to the third tower. See the top of page 107.

After we move the largest disk to the third tower, we are faced with a new problem. We now have a stack of disks which contains one fewer disks than the original (starting) stack and which resides on the second

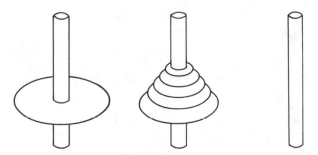

tower. All we have to do is find a way to move this stack to the third tower! We can forget the largest disk (which now rests on the third tower), since it will never move again.

We realize that we are faced with a new problem: We are to move a stack of N − 1 disks to the third tower (following the rules of course).

Here's what we have done so far:

We have moved N − 1 disks from the first tower to the second tower.

We have moved 1 disk (the largest) from the first tower to the third tower.

Now, we must move N − 1 disks from the second tower to the third tower, and we will be done.

Let us denote the task of moving N disks from tower one to tower three by the notation

MOVE (N, 1, 3)

Returning to the problem at hand, we recall that we have one disk on the third tower and N − 1 disks on the second tower. In order to move the bottom disk from the second tower to the third tower, we must reach another intermediate stage where we have only one disk on the second tower, only one disk (the very largest) on the third tower, and all the others on the first tower. We reached this stage in the four-coin problem after move number 11.

The point that we are making is that, in order to move N − 1 disks from one tower to another, we must make use of the tower that is empty as a sort of temporary holding place for the disks. That means that we will have to keep track of which tower is empty at each of the intermediate stages.

Now let us make a first attempt at writing a Pascal procedure to solve the puzzle. We will invent procedure MOVE as follows:

PROCEDURE MOVE(N, START, GOAL : INTEGER);
      BEGIN
             decide which tower is FREE (that is, which tower is empty)

move N − 1 disks to the FREE tower (if there is more than
1 disk here)

move 1 disk from the START tower to the GOAL tower

move N − 1 disks from the FREE tower to the GOAL
tower (again if there is more than one disk here)

END;

We will discuss each of these steps in turn. First, we number the towers
1, 2, and 3. Next we must decide which numbers designate the START,
FREE, and GOAL towers. START has all the disks on it at the beginning,
GOAL is where we want to put them, and the third one is FREE. GOAL
can represent an intermediate goal. We may want to move *all but one* disk
to a certain tower, so as to free up a third tower for the transfer of the
largest disk. In this case, if we start with all disks on tower 2 and desire to
move *all but one* of them to tower 1, then tower 1 is designated GOAL.
Now we must decide which tower is the FREE one. To do this, we use the
expression 6 minus START minus GOAL. The result is the number of the
FREE tower. In this instance, FREE := 6 − START − GOAL evaluates to
3, telling us that we must use the third tower as the FREE tower for this
move.

Now let us refine the above procedure a bit:

```
PROCEDURE MOVE (N, START, GOAL : INTEGER);
    BEGIN
        FREE := 6 − START − GOAL;
        IF N > 1 THEN MOVE (N − 1, START, FREE);
        WRITELN ('MOVE ONE DISK FROM TOWER',
            START,' TO TOWER ',GOAL);
        IF N > 1 THEN MOVE (N − 1, FREE,GOAL);
    END;
```

The IF tests are necessary for two reasons: they prevent attempting to
move zero disks from one tower to another, and they allow the procedure
to terminate eventually, when there are no more disks to be moved.

Exercise

1. With this background material, we ask you, the reader, to write a
    program that will print all of the moves necessary to solve the Towers
    of Hanoi puzzle for any number of disks. If you use a large number,
    you will find that this task quickly fills even very large computers to
    capacity, so we suggest that you limit your disks to 10 or fewer. The
    key line in the main program will be:

    MOVE (N, 1, 3);

10.0

Problems for solution

10.1   **ABOUT THE PROBLEMS**

Some of the problems in this chapter are pretty tough! Several depend on some knowledge of mathematics, but they are not essential to learning Pascal, and they are marked.

If you can handle all these problems, you have a much-better-than-average grasp of Pascal. They were designed to take hours or days—don't be discouraged. Since real-world problems rarely have all of the needed information in one place, neither do these problems. (Use of a dictionary can be very helpful in solving some of them.)

There are two sets of problems, actually, with 17 problems in each set. The problems that are labeled with an *E*, (such as Problem 1E) have a definite engineering flavor. Those problems with a *B* are of an entirely different type; they are suitable for those people who are interested in business applications of the computer. The problems that have an additional marking of *M* are essentially mathematical in nature, and they may safely be skipped without penalty if you need to. All the other problems just require common sense and perseverance.

The number of asterisks by a problem heading indicates its relative degree of difficulty. Problems with only one asterisk are almost trivial, and those with four or five asterisks are suitable for assignment as two-to-three-week projects.

The particular set of problems marked with an E happens to serve as an entire semester's homework for engineering computer science majors at the University of Oklahoma. Not one of several hundred students has managed to complete all 17! We mention this not to discourage you, but rather to *encourage* you, and provide problems that will eventually extend your capabilities further.

We present these problems for those people who sincerely desire and enjoy a challenge, and we would certainly enjoy receiving your letters and comments on these problems as you work on them.

Have fun!

10.2   PROBLEM SECTION

*   **Problem 1E**

You are to write a program that will provide you with a liter-gallon conversion chart for use in filling stations. This chart should show volume equivalents between liters and gallons and also allow conversion of price per liter to price per gallon and vice versa. You might try looking in the dictionary for conversion factors.

*   **Problem 1B**

You are to write a program that will make a table to convert interest rates per year to interest rates for various other periods. For example, it should be possible to look in your table and discover that 12 percent per year is 3 percent per quarter or 6 percent for six months.

*   **Problem 2EM**

Write a program that will produce a table of trigonometric sines, co-sines, secants, and cosecants. You may need a trig book for definitions, and you should include conversion from radians to degrees as part of your table. (* Needs trigonometry *)

*   **Problem 2B**

Write a program to show how much $1,000 will be worth in succeed-ing years if it is invested at 12 percent simple interest. Have your program make a table that can be read for any number of years from 1 to 10.

*   **Problem 3EM**

You are to write a program to provide a table of hyperbolic sines and hyperbolic cosines for integers from 0 to 180. You may find either an ele-mentary trigonometry book or an elementary calculus book handy for looking up definitions.

*   **Problem 3BM**

Write a program to make a table indicating how much $1,000 invested at 10 percent compounded annually will be worth each year for the next 10 years. A formula for accomplishing this task can be found in most be-ginning algebra books, or a little thinking will reveal a method to you. When this program is working, modify it so you can input from the keyboard any interest rate, any amount, and the number of compoundings per year.

---

*   **Problem 4E**

You are to prepare a table to convert degrees Fahrenheit degrees to degrees centigrade (Celsius) and vice versa. Your table should provide reasonable ranges and round off to the nearest degree for convenience. You may find several built-in Pascal functions useful.

---

*   **Problem 4B**

You are to prepare a table to show how much a given amount of money (say $1,000) will be worth in 10 years, if it is invested at interest rates which are compounded annually. Your table should provide for interest rates which vary from 6 percent (!) up to 25 percent (!!). Have the program round off results to the nearest dollar for convenience. You might look at the built-in Pascal function ROUND.

**   **Problem 5E**

You are to solve quadratic equations in all their possibilities, including complex root problems. You are to provide your program with a loop so that after it solves one quadratic equation it will ask you for another one. You will also have to provide a "stop flag" to cause the program to cease execution when there are no more equations to solve, and you will have to provide some method for entering a quadratic equation for solution. (* requires algebra *)

**   **Problem 5B**

Write a program that will accept the amount of a loan and its interest rate and determine the amount of an annuity that can be used to retire the debt after a certain period of time.

**   **Problem 6EM**

Write a program that uses Newton's method for solution of an equation that cannot be solved algebraically. An example of such a problem is

$$x * \sin(x) = 1$$

After you get your program working, try to solve

$$x = 2 \cos(x)$$

If you graph these equations, you will find a fundamental difference between them. Newton's method can be found in most beginning calculus texts.

** **Problem 6B**

Write a program to determine the average and standard deviation of a list of ages for applicants for loans. It is not necessary to retain all the ages in memory at once.

** **Problem 7EM**

You are to write a program that will integrate a certain function numerically. You may use the following integral if you like.

$$\int_0^1 (x^2 + x + 1)\, dx$$

After you have this working, try to integrate

$$\int_0^1 \sin^2(x)\, dx$$

There are several methods available, including brute force from the definition of definite integrals, or trapezoidal methods. We suggest that you use only a very basic method at this stage.

** **Problem 7B**

In a finance textbook, look up the *Rule of 78* (sometimes known as *sum-of-the-digits depreciation*). On the basis of this rule, write a program that will accept the amount of a loan, the length of the loan period, the interest rate, and the finance charge, and compute a table that indicates how much it will cost to pay the loan off early. If you like, you may assume a $5,000 loan with 36 payments spread over three years, with an interest rate of 15 percent, and a finance charge of $1,200. (These numbers are only approximate.)

After you have this table completed, add a column to it showing the actual interest rate paid if you pay the loan off early. For instance, if you pay off a 36-month loan at the end of the first month, you will actually pay the equivalent of 65 percent annual interest! Let your table go in one-month steps, showing costs if the loan is paid at the end of each month.

*** **Problem 8E**

Write a program that will solve two linear equations in two unknowns, providing for all possible cases.

***   **Problem 8B**

You are to be given two linear equations in two unknowns. One of these linear equations represents cost, and the other represents income. Write a program to find the break-even point. If there is no break-even point, you must so indicate.

***   **Problem 9EB**

(This problem is important for both engineering and business students.)

You are to sort a file of addresses so that people with the same last name will appear in zip-code order. An address consists of

      LASTNAME,FIRSTNAME,CITY,STATE,ZIPCODE

You may assume that each of these items starts in a particular column if it will make the program easier for you to write. You are to provide appropriate data to illustrate the features of your program. There are many sorting methods available. Several of the simplest include the *selection sort,* the *bubble sort,* and the *insertion sort.* You will certainly need to use arrays in this problem.

Hint: TYPE STRING = PACKED ARRAY [1..80] OF CHAR;

***   **Problem 10EB**

This problem is also appropriate for both business and engineering majors, since it illustrates a point of the Pascal language.

Write a program that will count the number of occurrences of each letter of the alphabet in a given text. Your summary must include, not only the number of occurrences of each character, but the total number of punctuation marks and the totals of small and capital letters. You should also indicate how many paragraphs and how many complete sentences occurred in the text.

***   **Problem 11EB**

This problem also illustrates a point of the language.

Write a program that will read a text and print the number of vowels that occurred and the number of consonants. The program should also count the occurrences of the word *the,* counting *THE, the,* and *The* as the same word but not counting such similar words as *thee.*

***   **Problem 12EB**

This program is intended to be useful, and it is likely to find its way into the personal "program library" of many people with diverse interests. It is also a challenging problem in its own right and a good exercise in use of arrays.

Write a program that will accept several paragraphs of text and justify (line up evenly) both the left and right margins. Paragraphs should be retained, and it should be possible to specify a line length. (One method of justification is to add blanks at certain places within a line.)

**** **Problem 13EM**

You are to manipulate complex numbers using record types and either functions or procedures.

You are to input either one or two complex numbers and an operation. You are to perform the operation and print the result. Repeat until the operation of E (for exit) is selected by the user of the program. The operations must include addition, subtraction, negation, multiplication, absolute value, division, conjugation, and for exit.

**** **Problem 13B**

Using record types, make a program that will (1) allow you to keep a list of employee names, addresses, hourly rates, number of hours worked, and base pay; (2) print a list of payroll deductions for each employee; and (3) print the appropriate weekly checks, with reports for the employees showing year-to-date totals for their deductions. Part of this problem is determining what deductions are appropriate for your particular set of employees. At the least, you should include appropriate deductions for withholding taxes.

**** **Problem 14EM**

You are to write a program to manipulate matrices, providing for the operations of addition, multiplication, subtraction, taking of determinants, and calculation of inverses if possible.

A study of recursive techniques will suggest that by using cofactors you can write a program that will invert any nonsingular square matrix of any size. It is probably more practical to limit your program to deal only with matrices of up to size three by three if you haven't studied linear algebra.

**** **Problem 14BM**

Write a program that will solve linear programming problems. Use this program to estimate how much of nutrients A, B, and C is required by a cow in order for her to gain weight at the rate of 1½ pounds a day at the lowest possible cost. You will have to research how such a problem should actually be worded before you can approach solving it with the computer. (This can become a problem of exceedingly large proportions.)

****   **Problem 15EB**

This problem is actually much easier than some of the previous problems, but it is presented at this time because it involves advanced concepts.

Write a program to manipulate a linked list, keeping the entries in ascending order. Operations must include printing of the contents of the list, addition of an item to the list, and deletion of an item from the list. This problem is important for students of all disciplines.

****   **Problem 16EB**

This problem is like the last one in that it is not as difficult as some of the previous problems but represents an advanced concept.

You are to manipulate a binary tree. Your program must use recursion and be capable of adding a node to a binary tree, listing the tree, or deleting a node from the tree. The case of an empty tree must be properly handled.

The Pascal User's Manual and Report by K. Jensen and N. Wirth gives part of this program. You may also want to consult any text on data structures.

*****   **Problem 17**

This problem is suitable for assignment as a term project for all disciplines.

This is the most difficult of the assigned problems, and it tends to be of large size. On the other hand, the resulting program may prove to be very useful. One simple approach to solving this problem is presented later in this book as a solved problem. You are encouraged to improve that program and modify it to fit your own personal needs.

By taking advantage of the previous problems, it is possible to accomplish this assignment with comparatively little effort.

You are to design and implement a "little black book" information system, which includes entries for name, address, city, state, zip code, phone number, and hair color.

Your program should allow searching for a particular entry on any field. For instance, it should be possible to search for all blonds or all persons with a certain zip code besides searching for a particular name. If you are feeling "cocky" you can provide a "near-miss" feature that will suggest entries that come closest to matching a specific request if an exact match is not found.

Additionally, you should be able to print a list of entries in ascending order, sorted on any of the fields.

Finally, you should be able to create disk files from the data which contain, for instance, all redheads, or all persons with the same last name.

Syntax diagrams and built-in features

A.1   WHAT IS SYNTAX?

Among other things, this appendix reveals to us the mystery of why certain semicolons appear where they do and other semicolons are missing. This appendix presents a description of the *syntax* of Pascal. That is, it gives the exact rules of formation for Pascal statements. By following these rules carefully, you will write programs that compile and run perfectly every time. There is no guarantee, however, that they will perform as you intended!

We need to have firmly in mind the difference between *syntax* and *logic*. The sentence "The sun comes up in the west" is syntactically correct. That is, it follows all of the rules of the English language for formation of sentences. The sentence is *logically* incorrect. The sun does not come up in the west.

In this appendix, we will find a description of the syntax of Pascal. It also includes *every* statement that is to be found in Pascal, including a few that we haven't met at all yet.

A.2   HOW TO READ SYNTAX DIAGRAMS

When learning a new language or using an obscure feature of an old one, programmers frequently have need to discover (or rediscover) just exactly how to write a particular statement. Minor misstatements can cause major problems, as all programmers know; so it is important to be able to express a statement exactly as it should be.

Syntax diagrams will not help the programmer select an appropriate statement to accomplish a particular task, but they will help him or her determine whether a particular sentence is correctly stated. In other words, the sentence "The sun comes up in the west" is syntactically correct, even though it is logically incorrect. Syntax diagrams deal with syntax, not logic. Logic is the programmer's job.

Working your way through syntax diagrams is a lot like working puzzles and can be about as much fun. With these diagrams, you can answer such questions as "When do I use a semicolon?" with surprising ease.

If you will refer to Figure A–1, we will try to explain how to use these tools.

Figure A–1

This diagram tells how to write a Pascal program. The words or symbols which appear in circles or ovals are required. Objects which appear in rectangles are defined in other syntax diagrams.

In order to write a legal program, just follow the arrows. For instance, the diagram above shows that, in order to write a program, we must first write the word PROGRAM followed by an identifier (which we have been calling the *program name*), followed by a required opening parenthesis, at least one more identifier (if there are several, they are separated by re-quired commas), a required closure of the parentheses, a required semi-colon, a block, and a required period.

What is a block, and what is an identifier? Each of these is described by its very own syntax diagram. Actually, the sequence of diagrams follows an order, but this order may not be apparent at first glance. The last pages of the syntax diagrams answer the tougher questions, while the first pages are devoted to developing the "building blocks" needed to make up the last diagrams. Each diagram can depend on the ones before it but not on the ones following it. Words appearing in CAPITAL letters are Pascal's key-words, and these are the words that we use to construct Pascal's state-ments.

By looking at the diagram of a block, it is easy to see where a semicolon should be used to separate different parts of a program.

If you follow the arrows through the syntax diagrams, you are guaran-teed a syntactically correct program. The logic of the same program is up to you, however.

As an example, consider the following program segment.

```
REPEAT
      STATEMENTA;
```

STATEMENTB;
STATEMENTC;   (* is this semicolon necessary ?*)
UNTIL. . . .

Is the semicolon at the end of STATEMENTC necessary? We will use the syntax diagram of a statement to find out. In Figure A—2 find the syntax diagram for a statement, and locate the REPEAT in the oval. Following the arrows, we find that we can have several statements within the body of the REPEAT . . . UNTIL . . ., but that the last one need not be followed by a semicolon, since we can reach the UNTIL without crossing a semi-colon in a circle or an oval.

Ok, then, I see that the semicolon is not necessary in this instance, but why does the program work if I do put one there?

Again, the answer can be found in the syntax diagram of a statement. If you follow the line all the way to the bottom, you can see that a statement can be "empty." That is, a statement can be made up of nothing!

Look again at STATEMENTC in the sample program segment. What we actually have is a "phantom statement" which follows the semicolon after STATEMENTC and comes before the UNTIL. This statement does nothing.

A similar analysis leads us to believe that the semicolon marked below is superfluous but harmless.

BEGIN
STATEMENTA;
STATEMENTB;
STATEMENTC;   (*this one*)
END;

If you are in doubt of this, look at the syntax for a statement (Figure A—2) and find the required words BEGIN and END. According to this, the sequence BEGIN . . . END; is perfectly legal, though it is somewhat use-less.

Incidentally, this same diagram can tell us how far we have progressed in our study of Pascal. There are only three statements that we have not yet studied, including the GOTO. Don't you wish it were really that easy?

A.3   THE REMAINING STANDARD SYNTAX DIAGRAMS

The syntax diagrams in Figure A—2 are copied from the original publi-cation of the *Pascal User's Manual and Report* by Niklaus Wirth and K. Jensen. The diagrams, along with the one appearing in section A.1 of this book, describe the entire Pascal language, as defined by its inventors.

If you find yourself getting confused, you may find it easier to start with the last diagram and work toward the first one, instead of the other way around.

**Figure A–2
Syntax diagrams**

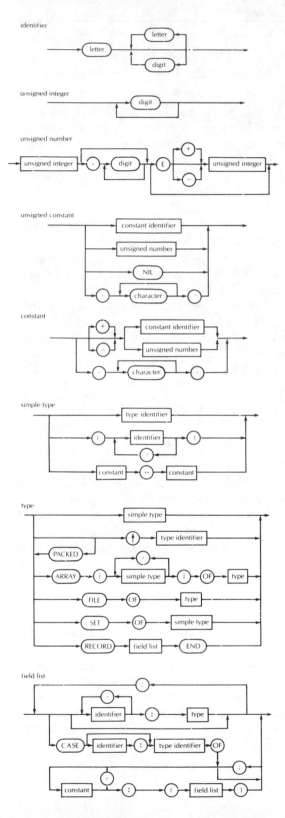

Figure A–2
(continued)

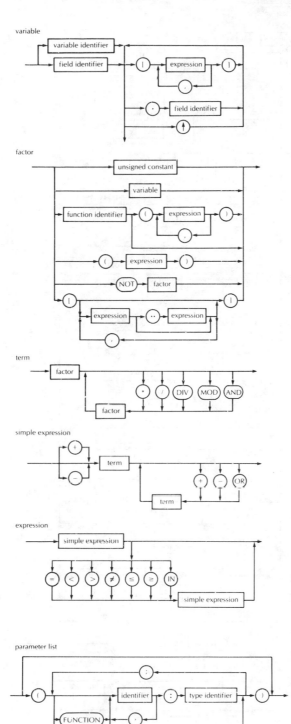

variable

factor

term

simple expression

expression

parameter list

**Figure A–2
(concluded)**

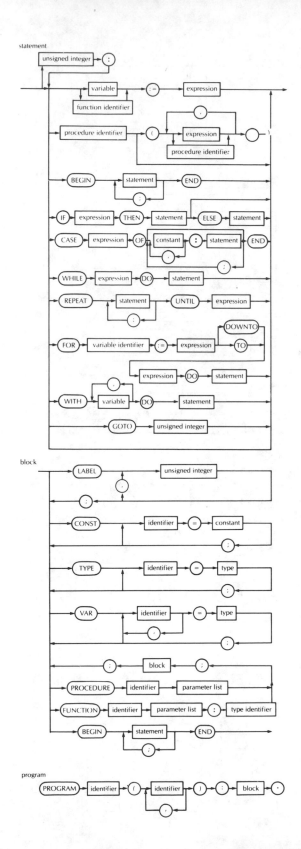

It is interesting to take some Pascal code segment that you have written and see if it meets all the requirements of a particular syntax diagram. If you do this, you may discover such items as superfluous semicolons scattered all over the place, or even find a better way to write the same code!

A.4   Pascal's BUILT-IN PROCEDURES AND FUNCTIONS

It is unfortunate that whenever computer languages are installed on different kinds of computers, it is sometimes necessary for compromises to be made. Although most computer manufacturers attempt to conform to some standard, not all of them implement all the features of the Pascal language. It is possible that some of the procedures and functions listed here will not work on your particular machine, even though we have included only those that are part of the standard definition of the language. Some implementations of Pascal offer powerful extensions including other procedures and functions beyond those presented here. The user's manual for your computer will surely provide a list of the procedures and functions valid for the machine.

Standard procedures

READ
READLN
WRITE
WRITELN
PUT
GET
RESET
REWRITE
PAGE
NEW
DISPOSE

Discussion.   READ, READLN, WRITE, and WRITELN were discussed in Section 2.2.5. Several options are available when one is using these procedures, and most of them have to do with utilizing external devices such as disk drives or printers. Consult the manual for your local installation.

PUT and GET are also intended for input and output operations. Their primary purpose is to deal with data other than the standard Pascal types of INTEGER, REAL, and CHAR. Their use involves knowing about such things as file pointers, which are often implemented in different ways on different machines.

RESET and REWRITE are used to direct output or input to external files, often disk files. In some systems, the REWRITE statement assists in using a printer.

The procedure PAGE can be used to cause an external printer to skip to the top of a new page or, in some installations, to clear a CRT screen.

Procedures NEW and DISPOSE were discussed in Section 8.4. They are used to deal with dynamic allocation of variables, and one often encounters installations where DISPOSE either does not work or gives an error message.

Some standard functions

ABS
SQR
SQRT
SIN
COS
EXP
LN
ARCTAN

Discussion.   ABS returns the absolute value of its argument. SQR returns the square of its argument, and SQRT returns the square root of its argument.

SIN and COS return the sine and cosine respectively of their arguments, and these functions expect arguments to be in radian measure. There is no standard tangent function, but it is easy to use trigonometric identities to construct the tangent and other usual trigonometric functions.

EXP returns the value of e raised to the power of the argument. LN is the natural logarithm function. Pascal has no exponentiation operator, but one can be constructed by using the following identity:

$$x = a^b = exp(b\ ln\ a)$$

The ARCTAN function returns the arc tangent of its argument. The resulting angle is measured in radians.

Other standard functions

ODD
EOF, EOLN
TRUNC
ROUND
ORD
CHR
SUCC
PRED

Discussion. ODD returns a Boolean value that is TRUE if the argument is an odd integer and FALSE if the argument is an even integer.

EOF returns a Boolean TRUE if the file pointer (used with external files, usually) is at the end of the file and a FALSE otherwise. This is often used in conjunction with RESET and a while statement that looks like this:

WHILE NOT EOF DO . . .

This function may be implemented in a nonstandard form by some computer manufacturers. It can be the source of much frustration if it is implemented in certain fashions. In its standard form it is both pleasurable and easy to use. EOLN is the "end of line" equivalent for detecting the end of an input line.

TRUNC removes the fractional part of a real number and returns an integer. For instance, TRUNC(3.94) is 3.

ROUND rounds a real number to the nearest integer. As an example, ROUND(3.94) is 4.

ORD and CHR are used to map scalar variables to integers and vice versa. They can also be used to send control codes to devices which could not ordinarily receive them because the keyboard does not have a key for the code. The set of integers utilized depends to some extent on the underlying character set for the particular computer in use.

PRED and SUCC were discussed in Chapter 6.

Some useful programs

B.1   PROBLEM SOLVING WITH Pascal

This appendix contains some of the author's most useful programs. They are designed to run under the UCSD Pascal system and may require some modification for other Pascal implementations.

Since the author is by profession a teacher and writer, some of these programs are designed to assist in those endeavors. The grade book systems have saved endless hours of time, the scheduling system has made some tasks possible that simply were not possible before, and the data base systems have served most admirably in several capacities, providing data bases for personal mailing lists, the books in my library, and the articles in my many journals and magazines, and indexing this text.

In some cases, several programs are used in conjunction with each other to form a system for accomplishing certain tasks. In these cases, the output of one program is often used as input for another program. This makes the programs small enough to run in most machines that feature a Pascal compiler. If the programs were not broken up in this fashion, it would require a large mainframe computer to run them. As it is, I am able to run all of them on my microcomputer with a single floppy disk drive.

If you concoct novel uses for some of these programs, please let me know. If you would like to consider sending me some of your programs for inclusion in the next printing of this book, I will be happy to consider your submissions.

Some of the following programs are written in capital letters, and some in lowercase. Most Pascal systems don't care, but if your system does care, you may find the first program useful.

127

B.2   GENERAL-PURPOSE SYSTEMS

B.2.1   Program DECAP

This program is very short. It is the result of the author's personal dissatisfaction with printed listings of programs that contain only uppercase letters.

When the author converted his personal computer system to a system that allowed lowercase letters, he was faced with two problems. The first problem was that programs that expected uppercase letters as input (per-

```
program decap (input,output);

    var disk,out : file of char;

        i,j : integer;

        infile,outfile,s,buffer : string;




begin
  writeln (' this program converts upper case');
  writeln (' only files to lower case only');
  writeln ('    the program converts all alpha-');
  writeln ('    betic information.');
  writeln;
  writeln;
  writeln (' what is the input file ');
  readln (infile);
  writeln (' what is the output file ');
  readln (outfile);

  reset (disk,infile);
  rewrite (out,outfile);

  while not eof(disk) do
    begin
     readln (disk,s);

     buffer := s;

     for i := 1 to length(s) do
       begin
        if ((s[i] <='Z') and (s[i] >= 'A')) then
           buffer[i] := chr(ord(s[i])+ord('a')-ord('A'));
       end;

      writeln (out,buffer);

    end;


  close (disk,lock);
  close (out,lock);
  end.
```

haps to drive a menu) would not function unless the operator shifted the keyboard into uppercase. The second problem was merely cosmetic: the author was offended by the appearance of traditional computer listings that printed uppercase only.

Program DECAP solved both problems. The program takes a program that was written in uppercase and converts it into lowercase letters. Only letters of the alphabet are affected, and other characters are left alone.

Use of this program depends on a couple of things. It is somewhat dependent on the underlying character set of your computer, and you must have a file system that will allow compilation of files that were created by other programs. (Most systems do this.) It is possible to modify DECAP to make it "RECAP" if necessary by changing the '+' and '−' signs about, and modifying the "IF".

B.2.2   Program BARGRAPH

Purpose.   This program takes a set of data and provides a bar graph of those data.

Usage.   The number of data items is set by NOVECTORS in the CONST section. SCREENWIDTH is normally 80 characters but may be different on your terminal. SCREENHEIGHT is 24 on many terminals but may be adjusted for your terminal. MAXLABEL gives the maximum length of a label that will be attached to the bottom of the graph.

How to use it.   Change the CONST section to suit your terminal. Then compile and run the program.

The program first asks for labels for each column of the bar graph. These labels may be typed in at the keyboard but must not exceed MAXLABEL in length.

Next, the program asks for data vectors. Just supply the numbers that you want to graph. The program will scale the data and provide a bar graph of them. The labels will appear on the columns, along with the value of the data for each column.

Suggested changes.   Modify the program to provide output to the printer instead of the screen. If you arrange the columns so that they are horizontal rather than vertical, you can put in lots more data points, at the expense of having to read the graph sideways. This problem is much easier than BARGRAPH, and I suggest that, to solve it, you start over instead of trying to modify BARGRAPH.

Bugs.   Using SCREENWIDTH $< 3*$NOVECTORS will cause trouble. Short screen heights are troublesome as well.

```
        program bargraph (input,output);

        (* This program is not very elegant...its purpose is to
           serve as an example of a program that is  almost
           totally dependent on its subprograms.  It is certainly
           possible to write this program in a more efficient
           fashion---although the present version will work on
           printers that are not capable of true graphics displays. *)


        const
              novectors = 8;
              (* change for a different number of data points *)

              screenwidth = 80;
              screenheight = 24;
              (* these should be adjusted for your terminal *)

              maxlabel = 10;


        var
              data, old : array [1..novectors] of real;
              height,zero, i : integer;
              lab : array [1..novectors,1..maxlabel] of char;

        procedure scale;
         var maxpos, maxneg, i : integer;

         begin
          maxpos := trunc(data[1]);
          maxneg := trunc(data[1]);

          for i := 1 to novectors do
            begin
             if trunc(data[i]) > maxpos then
               maxpos := trunc(data[i]);
             if maxneg > trunc(data[i]) then
               maxneg := trunc(data[i]);
            end;

          height := maxpos - maxneg + 2;
          zero := round(abs(maxneg) * (screenheight / height));

             (* now scale each point *)
          for i := 1 to novectors do
           data[i] := zero + round(data[i] / height * screenheight);

         end;  (* of scale *)



        procedure graph;
         var w,i,j : integer;

         begin
           w := screenwidth div novectors;

           for i := screenheight downto 1 do
            begin
             if i = zero then
              begin
               for j := 1 to screenwidth do
                write ('-');
               writeln;
              end
```

```
          else
           for j := 1 to novectors do
             begin
              if ( (i > zero) and (trunc(data[j]) > i) ) then
                 write ('***':w)
              else
               if ( (i < zero) and (trunc(data[j]) < i) ) then
                  write ('***':w)
               else
                write (' ':w)
             end; (* of the for-j loop  and the 'else' *)

           writeln;
          end; (* of the for-i loop *)

       end; (* of graph *)




procedure loaddata;
 begin
   for i := 1 to novectors do
     begin
       writeln (' data point number ',i);
       readln (data[i]);
       old[i] := data[i];
     end;
   end; (* of loaddata *)




procedure labels;
 var i,w,j : integer;


   begin
    w := screenwidth div novectors;

    writeln;
    for i := 1 to maxlabel do
     begin
      for j := 1 to novectors do
       write (lab[j,i]:w);
      writeln;
     end;

     writeln;
     for j := 1 to novectors do
      write (old[j]:w:1);
     writeln;
   end; (* labels *)



procedure getlabels;
 var i,j : integer;

 begin
   for j := 1 to novectors do
     begin
       for i := 1 to maxlabel do
```

```
        lab[j,i] := ' ';
      writeln;
      writeln;
      writeln (' give the label for point ',j);

      i := 1;
      while not eoln do
        begin
          read(lab[j,i]);
          i := i + 1;
        end;
        readln;
      end; (* of for-j *)

  end; (* of getlabels *)




  begin (* main program *)
    getlabels;
    loaddata;
    scale;
    graph;
    labels;
  end.
```

B.2.3   Program DITTO

Program DITTO acts like a ditto machine. For example, it takes a business letter and copies it as many times as you want. It can also put address information on the letters, if you like, and even print the mailing labels for the envelopes. If you do this, the letters are (of course) printed in Zip code order, so that you can take advantage of bulk mailing rates.

You will have to use the editor to create the two input files for DITTO.

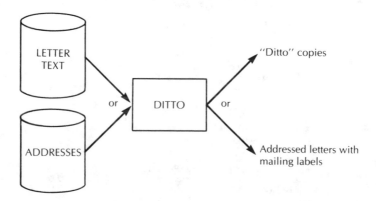

```
PROGRAM DITTO(INPUT,OUTPUT);

CONST PAGELENGTH = 66;
      MAXLETR = 66;
      MAXADR = 50;




VAR
   INDEX3,LINECNT,INDEX1,INDEX,
   LTRCNT,ADRLEN,COPYNBR,ADRCNT   : INTEGER;

   ADDRESS,LETTERNAME : STRING;

   LETTER :  ARRAY [1..MAXLETR] OF STRING;


   LINE :STRING;

   REPLY,REPLY1 : CHAR;

   DEV : FILE OF CHAR;


   NAME,ADR,CITYSTATE,ZIP : ARRAY [1..MAXADR] OF STRING;




PROCEDURE FORMFEED;
 BEGIN
  LINECNT:=LTRCNT+ADRLEN+1;
   FOR INDEX3:=LINECNT TO PAGELENGTH DO
    BEGIN
     WRITELN (DEV);
    END;
 END;


PROCEDURE WRITLETR;

 BEGIN
    FOR INDEX :=1 TO LTRCNT DO
     BEGIN
      WRITELN (DEV,LETTER[INDEX]);

     END;
    FORMFEED;
  END;




PROCEDURE READLETR;

 BEGIN

  WRITELN ('WHAT IS THE NAME OF THE TEXT?');
  READLN (LETTERNAME);
```

```
      RESET (DEV,LETTERNAME);

    LTRCNT:=0;

    WHILE NOT EOF(DEV) DO
     BEGIN
      READLN (DEV,LINE);
       IF NOT EOF(DEV) THEN
        BEGIN
         LTRCNT:=LTRCNT+1;
         LETTER[LTRCNT]:=LINE;
        END;
      END;
   CLOSE (DEV);
   WRITELN ('FINISHED READLETTER');

   END; (*OF READLETR*)



PROCEDURE READADDRESS;
 BEGIN
  ADRCNT:=0;
  WRITELN ('WHAT FILE CONTAINS THE ADDRESSES ?');
  READLN (ADDRESS);

   RESET (DEV,ADDRESS);

   WHILE NOT EOF(DEV) DO
    BEGIN
     ADRCNT:=ADRCNT+1;
     READLN (DEV,NAME[ADRCNT]);
     READLN (DEV,ADR[ADRCNT]);
     READLN (DEV, CITYSTATE[ADRCNT]);
     READLN (DEV,ZIP[ADRCNT]);
     READLN (DEV);

    END;

   CLOSE (DEV);
   ADRCNT:=ADRCNT-1;



   END;




PROCEDURE SORT;

 VAR TEMP : STRING;

      S,J,MIN : INTEGER;

      REPLY2 : CHAR;


 BEGIN (*OF SORT*)

  WRITELN ('DO YOU WANT TO SORT BY ZIP CODE OR NAME ?');
  READLN (REPLY2);
  WRITELN;

  FOR S:=1 TO ADRCNT DO
   BEGIN
    MIN:=S;

    FOR J:=S TO ADRCNT DO
```

```
    BEGIN
     CASE REPLY2 OF

      'Z': IF ZIP[J]<ZIP[MIN] THEN MIN:=J;

      'N': IF NAME[J]<NAME[MIN] THEN MIN :=J;

      END;(*CASE*)

    END; (*OF J LOOP*)

    (*NOW SWAP S NODE WITH MIN NODE*)

    TEMP:=NAME[MIN];NAME[MIN]:=NAME[S];NAME[S]:=TEMP;

    TEMP:=ADR[MIN];ADR[MIN]:=ADR[S];ADR[S]:=TEMP;

    TEMP:=CITYSTATE[MIN];CITYSTATE[MIN]:=CITYSTATE[S];CITYSTATE[S]:=TEMP;

    TEMP:=ZIP[MIN];ZIP[MIN]:=ZIP[S];ZIP[S]:=TEMP;

    (*END OF SWAP*)

  END;(*OF S LOOP*)

END;(*OF PROCEDURE SORT*)


PROCEDURE WRITLABEL;


  BEGIN

    WRITELN ('TURN ON PRINTER AND HIT RETURN');
    READLN (REPLY1);

    REWRITE (DEV,'PRINTER:');

    FOR INDEX:=1 TO ADRCNT DO
     BEGIN
      WRITELN (DEV,NAME[INDEX]);
      WRITELN (DEV,ADR[INDEX]);
      WRITELN (DEV,CITYSTATE[INDEX]);
      WRITELN (DEV,ZIP[INDEX]);
      WRITELN (DEV);
      WRITELN (DEV);
     END;

    CLOSE (DEV);

  END;




BEGIN (*MAIN PROGRAM*)

 REPEAT
  BEGIN
   WRITELN ('DITTO, ADDRESSOGRAPH, LABEL, OR QUIT ?');
   READLN (REPLY);

   CASE REPLY OF

     'L':  BEGIN
```

```
                        READADDRESS;
                         WRITLABEL;
                      END;

         'D':    BEGIN
                  ADRLEN:=0;
                  WRITELN;
                  WRITELN ('HOW MANY COPIES DO YOU WANT ?');
                  READLN (COPYNBR);
                  READLETR;
                  REWRITE (DEV,'PRINTER:');

                  FOR INDEX1:=1 TO COPYNBR DO WRITLETR;
                  CLOSE (DEV);
                 END;

         'A':    BEGIN
                  ADRLEN:=9;




                  READADDRESS;
                  WRITELN;
                  SORT;


                  READLETR;

                  REWRITE (DEV,'PRINTER:');


                  FOR INDEX1:=1 TO ADRCNT DO
                   BEGIN
                     BEGIN
                       WRITELN (DEV);
                       WRITELN (DEV);
                       WRITELN (DEV);
                       WRITELN (DEV);
                       WRITELN (DEV);
                       WRITELN (DEV,NAME[INDEX1]);
                       WRITELN (DEV,ADR[INDEX1]);
                       WRITELN (DEV,CITYSTATE[INDEX1]);
                       WRITELN (DEV,ZIP[INDEX1]);

                      END;

                    WRITLETR;
                   END;
                   CLOSE (DEV);

                   WRITELN ('DO YOU WANT TO GENERATE');
                   WRITELN ('ADDRESS LABELS ?');
                   READLN (REPLY1);

                   IF REPLY1='Y' THEN WRITLABEL;


                 END;


        END;

      END;

    UNTIL ( REPLY = 'Q');


   END.
```

B.3   A SCHEDULING SYSTEM

The schedule system is used to make student schedules from a list of student requests and available classes. The program recognizes that each classroom can only seat so many students, and it will allow students to sign up for a class at a particular hour only if the classroom is available. It makes every attempt to give students the classes they request at the hour that they request them. The system consists of three interdependent programs: SCHEDULE, KIDMAKER, and MAKECLASSSCHEDULE.

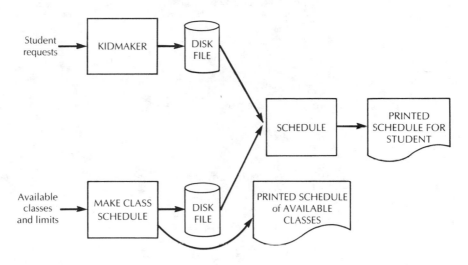

```
PROGRAM SCHEDULE (INPUT,OUTPUT);

CONST   MAXCLASS = 40;
        MAXTIME = 10;

VAR KID,NOKIDS,NOTIMES,
        MAXNBR,NOCLASSES,TIME,CLASS:INTEGER;

        FILLED : BOOLEAN;

        KIDNAME : STRING[40];

        SUBJECT : ARRAY [1..MAXCLASS] OF STRING[40];

        REQUEST : ARRAY [1..MAXCLASS] OF CHAR;

        CLASSAVAIL : ARRAY [1..MAXTIME,1..MAXCLASS] OF CHAR;

        CH:CHAR;

        MAXNO: ARRAY [1..MAXTIME,1..MAXCLASS] OF INTEGER;

        PRT,DSK:TEXT;

PROCEDURE LOADSUBJECTS;
```

```
      BEGIN
        RESET (DSK,'CLASSFILE.DATA');

        READLN (DSK,NOCLASSES);
        READLN (DSK,NOTIMES);

        FOR CLASS :=1 TO NOCLASSES DO
          BEGIN
            READLN (DSK,SUBJECT[CLASS]);
            READLN (DSK,MAXNBR);


            FOR TIME:=1 TO NOTIMES DO
              BEGIN
                READ (DSK,CLASSAVAIL[TIME,CLASS]);
                MAXNO[TIME,CLASS]:=MAXNBR;
              END;

            READLN (DSK);

          END;

        CLOSE (DSK,LOCK);

      END;(*OF LOADSUBJECTS*)


      (*MAIN PROGRAM*)

      BEGIN
        LOADSUBJECTS;
        WRITELN ('TURN ON PRINTER AND HIT RETURN');
        READLN (CH);
        REWRITE (PRT,'PRINTER:');


        RESET (DSK,'KIDFILE.DATA');
        READLN (DSK,NOKIDS);

        FOR KID:=1 TO NOKIDS DO
          BEGIN
            READLN (DSK,KIDNAME);

            FOR CLASS :=1 TO NOCLASSES DO READ (DSK,REQUEST[CLASS]);

            READLN (DSK);
            WRITELN (PRT);
            WRITELN (PRT);
            WRITELN (PRT,'SCHEDULE FOR ',KIDNAME);
            WRITELN (PRT);
            WRITELN (PRT,'  SUBJECTS REQUESTED: ');
            FOR CLASS :=1 TO NOCLASSES DO
              BEGIN
                IF REQUEST[CLASS] ='Y' THEN WRITE(PRT,'  ',SUBJECT[CLASS]);
              END;
            WRITELN (PRT);
            WRITELN (PRT);

            WRITELN (PRT,'SCHEDULE');
            WRITELN (PRT);

            FOR TIME :=1 TO NOTIMES DO
              BEGIN
                FILLED := FALSE;

                FOR CLASS :=1 TO NOCLASSES DO
                  BEGIN
                    IF ((CLASSAVAIL[TIME,CLASS] = 'Y')
                     AND (REQUEST[CLASS] = 'Y')
                     AND (MAXNO[TIME,CLASS] > 0)  AND (NOT  FILLED))
                    THEN
```

```
        BEGIN
         MAXNO[TIME,CLASS]:=MAXNO[TIME,CLASS]-1;
         REQUEST[CLASS]:='R';
         FILLED := TRUE;
         WRITELN (PRT,'TIME ',TIME,'   SUBJECT = ',SUBJECT[CLASS]);
        END;(*OF IF*)
      END;(*OF CLASS FOR*)
    END;(*OF TIME FOR*)

    WRITELN (PRT);


    WRITELN (PRT);
    WRITELN (PRT);
    WRITELN (PRT);
    WRITELN (PRT);
    WRITELN (PRT);

  END;(*OF KID FOR*)

 CLOSE(PRT);

 CLOSE (DSK,LOCK);

END.
```

```
PROGRAM KIDMAKER(INPUT,OUTPUT);

 CONST   MAXKIDS = 100;
         MAXREQUESTS = 10;

 VAR     KIDNAME: ARRAY [1..MAXKIDS] OF STRING[40];
         KIDREQUESTS : ARRAY [1..MAXKIDS,1..MAXREQUESTS] OF CHAR;

         KID : 1..MAXKIDS;
         REQ : 1..MAXREQUESTS;

         NOKIDS,CLASS : INTEGER;

         DSK : TEXT;


BEGIN (*MAKE THE KIDFILE*)
 FOR KID:=1 TO MAXKIDS DO
  BEGIN
   KIDNAME[KID]:='BLANK';
   FOR CLASS := 1 TO MAXREQUESTS DO
    KIDREQUESTS[KID,CLASS]:='N';
  END;


 KID:=1;

 WRITELN ('WHAT IS THE STUDENT NAME ?');
 WRITELN ('<ENTER "STOP" TO STOP>');

 READLN (KIDNAME[KID]);

 REPEAT
  BEGIN
   WRITELN (KIDNAME[KID],' REQUESTS WHAT SUBJECTS ?');
   WRITELN ('ENTER "0" TO STOP');

   REPEAT
    BEGIN
     WRITE ('SUBJECT NUMBER = ');
     READLN (CLASS);
     WRITELN;
     IF(( CLASS > 0) AND (CLASS <=MAXREQUESTS)) THEN KIDREQUESTS[KID,CLASS]:='Y';
    END;
```

```
   UNTIL CLASS = 0;

   KID:=KID +1;

   WRITELN ('NEXT KID <"STOP" TO STOP>');
   READLN (KIDNAME[KID]);
  END;
 UNTIL (KIDNAME[KID] = 'STOP');

(*WRITE IT TO KIDFILE*)


REWRITE (DSK,'KIDFILE.DATA');
 NOKIDS:=KID-1;

 WRITELN (DSK,NOKIDS);


FOR KID:=1 TO NOKIDS DO
 BEGIN
  WRITELN (DSK,KIDNAME[KID]);
  FOR CLASS :=1 TO MAXREQUESTS DO
   BEGIN
    WRITE (DSK,KIDREQUESTS[KID,CLASS]);
   END;

  WRITELN(DSK);
 END;


CLOSE (DSK,LOCK);

END.
```

```
PROGRAM MAKECLASSCHEDULE(INPUT,OUTPUT);

CONST MAXTIME = 10;
      MAXSUBJ = 40;


VAR    CLASS,TIME,NOCLASSES,NOTIMES : INTEGER;
       SUBJECT : ARRAY [1..MAXSUBJ] OF STRING[40];
       CLASSAVAIL : ARRAY [1..MAXTIME,1..MAXSUBJ] OF CHAR;

       MAXNO : ARRAY [1..MAXSUBJ] OF INTEGER;

       CH:CHAR;


       DSK: TEXT;



  PROCEDURE MAKEREPORT;
   BEGIN
    WRITELN ('TURN ON PRINTER AND HIT RETURN');

    READLN (CH);

    REWRITE (DSK,'PRINTER:');

    WRITELN (DSK,'FOLLOWING SCHEDULE IS AVAILABLE:');
    WRITELN (DSK);
    WRITELN (DSK);
    WRITELN (DSK);


    FOR CLASS :=1 TO NOCLASSES DO
      BEGIN
       WRITELN (DSK,SUBJECT[CLASS],' SUBJECT # ',CLASS,' MAX ENROLLMENT: ',
```

```
          MAXNO[CLASS],' AT TIMES:');
          WRITELN (DSK);
          FOR TIME :=1 TO NOTIMES DO
            IF CLASSAVAIL[TIME,CLASS] = 'Y' THEN
              WRITELN (DSK,'      ',TIME);
          WRITELN (DSK);
          WRITELN (DSK);
          WRITELN (DSK);
          WRITELN (DSK);
        END;

     CLOSE(DSK);
  END;(*OF MAKEREPORT*)


  (*MAIN PROGRAM TO MAKE CLASS SCHEDULE*)

  BEGIN


  WRITELN ('HOW MANY CLASSES ARE THERE ?');
  READLN (NOCLASSES);
  WRITELN ('HOW MANY TIMES ?');
  READLN (NOTIMES);

  FOR CLASS := 1 TO NOCLASSES DO
   BEGIN
     WRITELN ('CLASS NUMBER ',CLASS);
     WRITELN ('WHAT IS THE NAME OF THE SUBJECT ?');
     READLN (SUBJECT[CLASS]);
     WRITELN ('HOW MANY STUDENTS CAN THIS CLASS HOLD ?');
     READLN (MAXNO[CLASS]);


     WRITELN;
     WRITELN ('IS THIS CLASS AVAILABLE AT:');
     WRITELN ('ANSWER "Y" OR "N"');
     WRITELN;

     FOR TIME :=1 TO NOTIMES DO
      BEGIN
        WRITELN ('TIME SLOT # ',TIME,' ? <Y OR N >');
        READLN (CLASSAVAIL[TIME,CLASS]);
       END;
   END;


   (*WRITE OUT TO CLASSFILE.TEXT*)

   WRITELN;
   WRITELN;
   WRITELN ('STANDBY...CREATING CLASSFILE');
   WRITELN;
   WRITELN;


   REWRITE (DSK,'CLASSFILE.DATA');

   WRITELN (DSK,NOCLASSES);
   WRITELN (DSK,NOTIMES);

   FOR CLASS := 1 TO NOCLASSES DO
    BEGIN
      WRITELN (DSK,SUBJECT[CLASS]);
      WRITELN (DSK,MAXNO[CLASS]);

      FOR TIME :=1 TO NOTIMES DO
       WRITE(DSK,CLASSAVAIL[TIME,CLASS]);
      WRITELN(DSK);

    END;
```

```
CLOSE(DSK,LOCK);

(*NOW MAKE REPORT*)

MAKEREPORT;


END.
```

B.4   GRADING SYSTEMS

B.4.1   Grading system one

We present here two approaches to keeping track of grades. The first consists of programs GRADBOOK, MIDTERM, and ENDOFYEAR. GRAD-BOOK can perform all the duties of a standard grade book, such as add a student to a class, change grades, add grades, and produce averages. MID-TERM can be used to manually enter grades for a one-shot grade report, while ENDOFYEAR is used to generate for the teacher a report which even curves the grades.

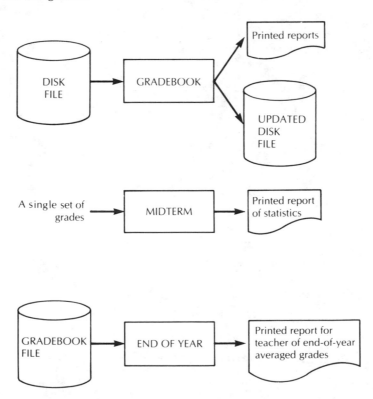

```
PROGRAM MIDTERM(INPUT,OUTPUT);


TYPE
    STUDENT = RECORD
                 NAME : STRING[40];
                 GRADES : ARRAY [1..15] OF REAL;
                 TOTAL : REAL;
                 END;

VAR
    NBR,NBRGRADES,SAVE,INDEX, INDEX1 : INTEGER;
    TEMP : STUDENT;
    KID : ARRAY [1..45] OF STUDENT;
    POSSIBLE,AVERAGE : REAL;
    CH,LETTER :CHAR;
    DEV : FILE OF CHAR;




PROCEDURE SORT;
 BEGIN
  FOR INDEX:=1 TO NBR DO
    BEGIN
     SAVE:= INDEX;
     FOR INDEX1:=INDEX TO NBR DO
       BEGIN
        IF KID[SAVE].TOTAL <= KID[INDEX1].TOTAL
          THEN SAVE := INDEX1;
       END;

      TEMP := KID[SAVE];
      KID[SAVE]:=KID[INDEX];
      KID[INDEX]:=TEMP;
    END;
 END;


PROCEDURE PRINTIT;
 PROCEDURE CURVIT;
  VAR NO : REAL;
    BEGIN
     IF (AVERAGE < 0.7*POSSIBLE) THEN
      NO:=AVERAGE / 0.7
     ELSE NO := POSSIBLE;

     IF (KID[INDEX].TOTAL >=  0.9*NO ) THEN
      LETTER:='A'
     ELSE
      IF KID[INDEX].TOTAL >= 0.8 * NO THEN
      LETTER:='B'
      ELSE
       IF KID[INDEX].TOTAL >= 0.7 * NO THEN
       LETTER:='C'


      ELSE
       IF KID[INDEX].TOTAL >= 0.6*NO THEN
       LETTER:='D'
       ELSE LETTER:='F';
   END;

BEGIN
 WRITELN ('TURN ON PRINTER AND HIT RETURN');
 READLN (CH);

 REWRITE (DEV,'PRINTER:');

 ·IF (AVERAGE >= 0.7 * POSSIBLE) THEN
```

```
        WRITELN (DEV,'NO CURVE FOR THESE GRADES');
        WRITELN(DEV);
        WRITELN (DEV);
        WRITELN (DEV);

   FOR INDEX:=1 TO NBR DO
    BEGIN
     WITH KID[INDEX] DO
      BEGIN
       WRITELN (DEV);
       WRITELN (DEV);
       WRITELN (DEV,NAME,'  TOTAL = ',TOTAL:5:1,'  RANK IS ',INDEX);
       CURVIT;
       WRITELN (DEV,'YOUR CURVED GRADE IS ',LETTER,'  CLASS AVE IS ',AVERAGE:5:1);
       FOR INDEX1:=1 TO NBRGRADES DO
        WRITE (DEV,'   ',GRADES[INDEX1]:5:1);
       WRITELN(DEV);
      END;
    END;
  CLOSE(DEV);
 END;


PROCEDURE CLASSAVE;
 BEGIN
  AVERAGE:=0.0;
  FOR INDEX:=1 TO NBR DO
   AVERAGE:=AVERAGE + KID[INDEX].TOTAL;
  AVERAGE:=AVERAGE/(NBR);
 END;


BEGIN (*MAIN*)
 WRITELN ('HOW MANY KIDS IN CLASS ?');
 WRITELN ('  (MAX IS 45) ');
 READLN (NBR);
 WRITELN ('HOW MANY GRADES PER KID ?');
 WRITELN (' (MAX IS 15) ');
 READLN (NBRGRADES);
 WRITELN (' WHAT IS THE HIGHEST POSSIBLE TOTAL ');
 READLN (POSSIBLE);
 WRITELN;
 FOR INDEX:=1 TO NBR DO


   BEGIN
    WITH KID[INDEX] DO
     BEGIN
      WRITELN;
      WRITELN ('NAME ');
      READLN (NAME);
      WRITELN ('GIVE ',NBRGRADES,'  GRADES');
      WRITELN ('ONE TO A LINE ');
      WRITELN;
      FOR INDEX1:=1 TO NBRGRADES DO
        READLN (GRADES[INDEX1]);

      CH:='N';

      REPEAT
       BEGIN
        WRITELN;
        WRITELN ('ARE ALL THESE CORRECT ?');
        READLN (CH);

        IF CH = 'N' THEN
         BEGIN
          WRITELN;
          WRITELN ('FIX WHICH GRADE ?');
```

```
                        READLN (INDEX1);
                        WRITELN ('GIVE CORRECT GRADE ');
                        READLN (GRADES[INDEX1]);
                        WRITELN;
                        WRITELN ('CORRECTED GRADES:');
                        FOR INDEX1:=1 TO NBRGRADES DO
                          WRITELN (INDEX1,'   ',GRADES[INDEX1]:5:1);
                        WRITELN;
                      END;

                END;
                UNTIL CH = 'Y';

                TOTAL := 0;
                FOR INDEX1 := 1 TO NBRGRADES DO
                  TOTAL := TOTAL + GRADES[INDEX1];

            END;
          END;

      CLASSAVE;
      SORT;
      PRINTIT;
      END.
```

```
PROGRAM GRADBOOK (INPUT,OUTPUT);

CONST NOSTUD = 50;
      NOGRAD = 10;


TYPE STUDENT = RECORD
                  SSN : STRING;
                  NAME:STRING;
                  NBR: INTEGER;
                  LETTER:STRING;
                  GRADE: ARRAY [1..NOGRAD] OF REAL;
               END;




VAR DISK : FILE OF STUDENT;
    WORK: ARRAY [1..NOSTUD] OF STUDENT;
    IDNBR,REPLY,FILENAME:STRING;

    J,COUNT,I,INDEX,TEST:INTEGER;

    GRD,AVERAGE,TOTAL:REAL;

    STOP,QUIT:BOOLEAN;

    DEV : TEXT;


    REPLY3,REPLY1:CHAR;



PROCEDURE DISKLOAD;
 BEGIN
   WRITELN ('WHAT IS THE NAME OF THE DISK FILE TO BE LOADED?');
   READLN (FILENAME);
   RESET (DISK,FILENAME);
   COUNT:=0;
```

```
WHILE NOT EOF(DISK) DO
 BEGIN
  COUNT:=COUNT+1;
  WORK[COUNT]:=DISK^;
  GET(DISK);
 END;

CLOSE (DISK,LOCK);

WRITELN ('THERE ARE ',COUNT,' ITEMS IN THE DATA BASE');


 END; (*OF DISKLOAD*)




 PROCEDURE DISKSAVE;
  BEGIN
   REWRITE (DISK,FILENAME);

   FOR I:=1 TO COUNT DO
    BEGIN
     IF WORK[I].SSN<>' ' THEN BEGIN DISK^:=WORK[I];PUT(DISK);END;
    END;

   CLOSE (DISK,LOCK);

  END;(*OF DISKSAVE*)




 PROCEDURE ADD;
  BEGIN
   COUNT:=COUNT+1;
   WRITE('STUDENT SSN = ');
   READLN (WORK[COUNT].SSN);
   WRITE ('STUDENT NAME: ');
   READLN (WORK[COUNT].NAME);
   WORK[COUNT].NBR:=0;
   WORK[COUNT].LETTER:=' ';
   FOR J:=1 TO NOGRAD DO WORK[COUNT].GRADE[J]:=0;
  END; (*OF ADD*)



FUNCTION TESTAVE:REAL;

 BEGIN
  WRITELN (' WHICH TEST DO YOU WANT TO AVERAGE ?');
  READLN (TEST);

  TOTAL:=0;
  FOR I:=1 TO COUNT DO
   BEGIN
    IF WORK[I].LETTER=' ' THEN TOTAL:=TOTAL+WORK[I].GRADE[TEST];
   END;

  TESTAVE:=TOTAL/COUNT;

 END; (*OF FUNCTION TESTAVE*)




 PROCEDURE TSTADD;
```

```
     BEGIN
      WRITELN ('THIS IS TEST NUMBER ',WORK[1].NBR+1);
      WRITELN;

      FOR I:=1 TO COUNT DO
       BEGIN
        WITH WORK[I] DO
         BEGIN
          NBR:=NBR+1;
          WRITE (SSN,'  ',NAME,'  GRADE = ');
          READLN (GRADE[NBR]);
          WRITELN;

         END;
       END; (*OF FOR*)

      WRITELN;
      WRITELN;

     END; (*OF TSTADD*)


   PROCEDURE CREATE;
    BEGIN
     WRITELN ('WHAT IS THE CLASSFILE TO BE CALLED?');
     READLN (FILENAME);
     WRITELN ('HOW MANY STUDENTS WILL THERE BE ?');
     READLN (COUNT);

     FOR I:=1 TO COUNT DO
      BEGIN
       WITH WORK[I] DO
        BEGIN
         WRITELN;
         WRITE ('SSN= ');
         READLN (SSN);
         WRITE ('NAME: ');
         READLN (NAME);
         WRITELN;
         NBR:=0;
         LETTER:=' ';
         FOR J:=1 TO NOGRAD DO GRADE[J]:=0;
        END;
      END; (*OF FOR*)

     WRITELN ('DISK SAVE FOLLOWS-STANDBY...');
     DISKSAVE;

    END; (*OF CREATE*)

   FUNCTION STUAVE(N:INTEGER):REAL;

    VAR I:INTEGER;
    BEGIN


      WITH WORK[N] DO
       BEGIN
        AVERAGE:=0;

        FOR I:=1 TO NBR DO
         BEGIN
          AVERAGE:=AVERAGE+GRADE[I];
         END;

        IF NBR>0 THEN STUAVE:=AVERAGE/NBR ELSE
          STUAVE:=0;
```

```
        END;

     END;  (* OF FUNCTION STUAVE*)



  FUNCTION CLASSAVE:REAL;

   VAR I,CNT:INTEGER;
   BEGIN
    TOTAL:=0;
    CNT:=0;

    FOR I:=1 TO COUNT DO
     BEGIN
       IF WORK[I].LETTER=' ' THEN
        BEGIN
         CNT:=CNT+1;
         TOTAL:=TOTAL+STUAVE(I);
        END;
     END;

     IF CNT>0 THEN CLASSAVE:=TOTAL/CNT
       ELSE CLASSAVE:=0;

   END;  (*OF FUNCTION CLASSAVE*)




  PROCEDURE STUREPT(INDEX:INTEGER);
  VAR I:INTEGER;

  BEGIN
   WITH WORK[INDEX] DO
    BEGIN
      WRITELN (SSN,' ',NAME,'    AVE= ',STUAVE(INDEX):5:2,'    ',LETTER);
      WRITELN;
      WRITELN ('SCORES ARE :');WRITELN;

      FOR I:=1 TO NBR DO WRITE (I,':',GRADE[I]:5:2,'   ');


      WRITELN;
      WRITELN;
      WRITELN;
      WRITELN;
      WRITELN;
     END;

  END;  (*OF STUDENT REPORT*)



  PROCEDURE INQUIRY;(*MAJOR PROCEDURE*)

   PROCEDURE CHANGESCORE;
    BEGIN
     WRITE ('WHICH SCORE ?');
     READLN (I);
     WRITE ('NEW GRADE ',I,' = ');
     READLN (WORK[INDEX].GRADE[I]);
     STUREPT(INDEX);
    END; (*OF CHANGESCORE*)
```

```
PROCEDURE DROP;
  BEGIN
    WRITELN ('DROP PASSING (P) OR FAILING (X)');
    READLN (REPLY);
    WORK[INDEX].LETTER:=REPLY;
  END;(*OF DROP*)




BEGIN (*OF MAIN PART OF INQUIRY*)
  WRITELN ('WHAT IS THE SSN OF THE STUDENT?');
  READLN (IDNBR);
  STOP:=FALSE;
  INDEX:=O;

  FOR I:=1 TO COUNT DO
   BEGIN
    IF WORK[I].SSN=IDNBR THEN INDEX:=I;
   END;

  IF INDEX>O THEN
   BEGIN
    STUREPT(INDEX);

     REPEAT
     WRITELN ('DO YOU WANT TO :');
     WRITELN (' <C> CHANGE A SCORE');
     WRITELN (' <D> DROP THE STUDENT');
     WRITELN (' <R> REINSTATE THE STUDENT');
     WRITELN (' <E> EXIT FROM INQUIRY');



     WRITELN;
     READLN (REPLY3);
       BEGIN
        CASE REPLY3 OF
          'C':CHANGESCORE;
          'D':DROP;
          'R':WORK[INDEX].LETTER:=' ';
          'E':STOP:=TRUE;
         END;

      END;

   UNTIL (STOP=TRUE);

END;



END;(*OF INQUIRY*)


PROCEDURE PRTRPTS;
 VAR I:INTEGER;
 PROCEDURE YEARTODATE;
  BEGIN
   FOR I:=1 TO COUNT DO
    WITH WORK[I] DO
     BEGIN
      WRITELN(DEV);
WRITELN (DEV,SSN,'   ',NAME,'  GRADE = ',LETTER,'  AVERAGE = ',STUAVE(I):5:2);
      WRITELN(DEV);
     END;
  END; (*OF YEARTODATE*)
```

```
PROCEDURE FINAL;
 VAR I:INTEGER;
 BEGIN
  FOR I:=1 TO COUNT DO
   BEGIN
    WITH WORK[I] DO
     BEGIN
      IF (LETTER=' ') THEN
       BEGIN
        GRD:=STUAVE(I);
        IF GRD<=100 THEN LETTER:='A';
        IF GRD<90 THEN LETTER:='B';
        IF GRD<80 THEN LETTER:='C';
        IF GRD<70 THEN LETTER:='D';
        IF GRD<60 THEN LETTER:='F';
       END;
     END;
   END;
  YEARTODATE;
 END;(*OF FINAL*)




  PROCEDURE STUDS;(*PART OF PRTRPTS*)
   VAR INDEX,J:INTEGER;
   BEGIN
    FOR INDEX:=1 TO COUNT DO
     BEGIN
      WITH WORK[INDEX] DO
       BEGIN
        WRITELN (DEV);
        WRITELN (DEV);
        WRITELN (DEV,SSN,'  ',NAME,'  ',LETTER,'  ',STUAVE(INDEX):5:2);
        WRITELN (DEV);
        WRITELN (DEV, 'SCORES : ');
        FOR J:=1 TO NBR DO
         WRITE (DEV,J,':',GRADE[J]:5:1,'   ');
        WRITELN (DEV);
        WRITELN (DEV);
       END;
     END; (*OF FOR*)
   END;(*OF STUDS*)



BEGIN (*MAIN PART OF PRTRPTS*)
 WRITELN ('TURN ON PRINTER AND HIT RETURN ');
 READLN (REPLY3);

 REWRITE (DEV,'PRINTER:');

 STOP:=FALSE;
 REPEAT
  WRITELN ('DO YOU WANT:');
  WRITELN (' <S>:  REPORTS FOR STUDENTS');
  WRITELN (' <Y>:  YEAR TO DATE FOR INSTRUCTOR');
  WRITELN (' <F>:  FINAL REPORT FOR INSTRUCTOR');
  WRITELN (' <Q>:  QUIT PRINTED REPORTS');

  READLN (REPLY1);

  CASE REPLY1 OF
      'S':  STUDS;
      'Y':  YEARTODATE;
      'F':  FINAL;
      'Q':  STOP:=TRUE;
     END;
UNTIL (STOP=TRUE);
```

```
        CLOSE (DEV);

   END; (*OF PRINTED REPORTS*)


   BEGIN (*MAIN PROGRAM*)
     QUIT:=FALSE;

     REPEAT
       WRITELN ('<C>: CREATE NEW CLASS');
       WRITELN ('<A>: ADD STUDENT TO CURRENT CLASS');
       WRITELN ('<I>: INQUIRY AND UPDATE');
       WRITELN ('<T>: ENTER NEW TEST SCORES');
       WRITELN ('<L>: LOAD CLASS FROM DISK');
       WRITELN ('<S>: SAVE WORKFILE TO DISK');
       WRITELN ('<Q>: QUIT PROCESSING');
       WRITELN ('<R>: CLASS TEST AVERAGE');
       WRITELN ('<P>: PRINTED REPORTS');


       READLN (REPLY1);
        CASE REPLY1 OF
           'C':   CREATE;
           'A':   ADD;
           'I':   INQUIRY;
           'T':   TSTADD;
           'L':   DISKLOAD;
           'S':   DISKSAVE;
           'Q':   QUIT:=TRUE;
           'R':   WRITELN(TESTAVE);
           'P':   PRTRPTS;

         END;

     UNTIL (QUIT=TRUE);

   END.
```

```
PROGRAM ENDOFYEAR (INPUT,OUTPUT);

CONST NOSTUD = 50;
      NOGRAD = 10;


TYPE STUDENT = RECORD
                 SSN : STRING;
                 NAME:STRING;
                 NBR: INTEGER;
                 LETTER:STRING;
                 GRADE: ARRAY [1..NOGRAD] OF REAL;
               END;




VAR DISK : FILE OF STUDENT;
    WORK: ARRAY [1..NOSTUD] OF STUDENT;
    FILENAME:STRING;

    INDEX,COUNT,I:INTEGER;

    HOME,EXTRA,MIN,AVERAGE,TOTAL:REAL;


    REPLY:CHAR;

    DEV : TEXT;
```

```
PROCEDURE DISKLOAD;
 BEGIN
  WRITELN ('WHAT IS THE NAME OF THE DISK FILE TO BE LOADED?');
  READLN (FILENAME);
  RESET (DISK,FILENAME);
  COUNT:=0;

  WHILE NOT EOF(DISK) DO
   BEGIN
    COUNT:=COUNT+1;
    WORK[COUNT]:=DISK^;
    GET(DISK);
   END;

  CLOSE (DISK,LOCK);

  WRITELN ('THERE ARE ',COUNT,' ITEMS IN THE DATA BASE');

 END; (*OF DISKLOAD*)




PROCEDURE REPORT;

 BEGIN
  WITH WORK[INDEX] DO
   BEGIN
    HOME:=(GRADE[5]+GRADE[6])/2.0;
    EXTRA:=GRADE[7];
    MIN:=100;
    TOTAL:=0;

    FOR I:=1 TO 4 DO
     BEGIN
      TOTAL:=TOTAL+GRADE[I];
      IF GRADE[I]<MIN THEN MIN:=GRADE[I];
     END;

    IF HOME<MIN THEN MIN:=HOME;

    TOTAL:=TOTAL+EXTRA+HOME-MIN+GRADE[8];
    AVERAGE:=TOTAL/5.0;
   END;
 END;

(*OF PROCEDURE REPORT*)


BEGIN (*MAIN PROGRAM*)


 DISKLOAD;
 WRITELN ('TURN ON PRINTER AND HIT RETURN');
 READLN (REPLY);

 REWRITE (DEV,'PRINTER:');


 FOR INDEX:=1 TO COUNT DO
  BEGIN
   REPORT;
   WITH WORK[INDEX] DO
   BEGIN
   WRITELN (DEV,'NAME: ',NAME);
   WRITELN (DEV);
   WRITELN (DEV,'TEST SCORES ARE: ');
   WRITELN (DEV,GRADE[1]:5:2,'  ',GRADE[2]:5:2,'  ',GRADE[3]:5:2,'  ',GRADE[4]:5:2);
   WRITELN (DEV);
```

```
      WRITELN (DEV,'PROGRAM GRADES ARE: ',GRADE[5]:5:2,'   ',GRADE[6]:5:2);
      WRITELN (DEV);


      WRITELN (DEV,'LOWEST SCORE IS ',MIN:5:2);
      WRITELN (DEV);
      WRITELN (DEV,'EXTRA PROGRAM WORK IS ',GRADE[7]:5:2);
      WRITELN (DEV);
      WRITELN (DEV,'GRADE ON FINAL EXAM :   ',GRADE[8]:5:2);
      WRITELN (DEV);
      WRITELN (DEV,'STUDENT AVERAGE IS ',AVERAGE:5:2);
      WRITELN (DEV);
      WRITELN (DEV);
      WRITELN (DEV);
      WRITELN (DEV);
      WRITELN (DEV);
      WRITELN (DEV);
    END; (*OF WITH DO*)
  END; (*OF FOR-DO*)

  CLOSE (DEV);

END. (*OF PROGRAM*)
```

B.4.2   Grading system two

The three programs FILES, DATAINQ, and SUMMARY represent a "slicker" and more full-featured grade book system than do the previous programs. The central core of this system is the notion that programs can share data files, and if they do so, they must each produce files that are compatible with the other two programs.

Each program in the system has a different purpose. Program FILES is used to create new class files or to add test scores to existing class files or even to add a student to an existing class file.

Program DATAINQ is used to inspect and update existing class files. If you want information about a particular student you should use DATAINQ. Using this program you can drop or reinstate students in a class, correct incorrectly recorded grades, or get a printout of an individual student's records. You can search either by ID number or by name. There is also a "browse" feature that lets you wander through the gradebook at will.

Program SUMMARY is used by the instructor to get summary information from the grade book. What was the average of quiz three? What is the class average? SUMMARY can tell you. If you want a graph of test scores, such as a histogram, you can use SUMMARY for this purpose. Finally, you can create printed reports that make it easy to determine a student's grade based on his or her class standing.

This grade book system does some things differently than the previous system did. It is a little harder to use, but it can do some things that the other system can't, and vice versa. A good exercise would be to combine the "best of both" into a single system.

```
program files (input,output);

const nostud =  50;
      nograd = 20;


type student = record
                 ssn,name,comment:string;
                 letter:char;
                 grade: array [0..nograd] of real;
               end;




var disk : file of char;
    kid: array [0..nostud] of student;
    nbr,j,count,i:integer;

    ch,ch1,ch2,ch3: char;

    filename:string;

    stop : boolean;




procedure diskload;
 begin
  writeln;
  writeln ('what is the name of the class ');
  writeln (' file ?');
  readln (filename);
  writeln (' ------standby------');
  reset (disk,filename);
  count:= 0;

  while not eof(disk) do
   begin
    read(disk,kid[count].letter);
    readln (disk,kid[count].ssn);
    readln (disk,kid[count].name);
    readln (disk,kid[count].comment);

    for j := 0 to nograd do
     begin
      read (disk,kid[count].grade[j]);
      if ((j > 0) and (j mod 12 = 0)) then readln (disk);
     end;


   if nograd mod 12 <> 0 then readln (disk);
   count:=count+1;
  end;

 close (disk,lock);

 count := count -1;
 writeln;
 writeln ('there are ',count,' items in the data base');
 writeln;

end; (*of diskload*)
```

```
procedure disksave;
 begin
  writeln (' standby...writing to disk');
  rewrite (disk,filename);

  for i:=0 to count do
   begin
   write(disk,kid[i].letter);
   writeln (disk,kid[i].ssn);
   writeln (disk,kid[i].name);
   writeln (disk,kid[i].comment);

   for j := 0 to nograd do
    begin
     write (disk,kid[i].grade[j]:6:1);
     if ((j > 0) and (j mod 12 = 0)) then writeln(disk);
    end;

   if nograd mod 12 <> 0 then writeln (disk);
   end;

  close (disk,lock);

 end;(*of disksave*)




procedure add;
 begin
  repeat
   writeln;
   write('student ssn = ');
   readln (kid[count].ssn);
   write ('student name: ');
   readln (kid[count].name);
   write ('comment :');
   readln (kid[count].comment);


   writeln ('correct ? (<cr> or "n")');
   readln (ch);
   writeln;

   if ch = 'n' then write (' re-enter');
  until ch <> 'n';
  kid[count].letter:=' ';
  for j:=0 to nograd do kid[count].grade[j]:=-1;
 end; (*of add*)




procedure tstadd;
 var nue : integer;

 begin
  writeln;
  writeln;
  writeln ('***warning***');
  writeln;
  writeln (' it is possible to destroy an old');
  writeln (' test grade by giving the wrong');
  writeln (' answer to this question...');
  writeln (' you have already entered test numbers:');
```

```
       for nue := 1 to nograd do
        if kid[0].grade[nue]>=0 then
         write (' ',nue);
       writeln;

       writeln;
       writeln (' which test number do you want to add ?');
       readln (nbr);

       writeln (' what is the relative weight of this test?');
       writeln;
       readln (kid[0].grade[nbr]);
       writeln;
       writeln;

       for i:=1 to count do
        begin
         with kid[i] do
          begin
           repeat
            writeln;
            write (ssn,' ',name,'  grade = ');
            readln (grade[nbr]);
            writeln;
            writeln ('correct ? (<cr> or "n")');
            readln (ch2);
            if ch2 = 'n' then write ('re-enter');
           until ch2 <> 'n';


          end;
        end; (*of for*)

       writeln;
       writeln;

      end; (*of tstadd*)


   procedure create;
    begin
     writeln;
     writeln ('what is the classfile to be called?');
     readln (filename);
     writeln;
     writeln (' you are to give the student''s');
     writeln (' id number and name, and any comment');
     writeln (' that you care to make.  when you');
     writeln (' are done, just answer each question');
     writeln (' with "last"');
     writeln;

      count := 1;
      repeat
          writeln;
          add;
          count := count + 1;
      until kid[count-1].name = 'last';

      count := count -2;


      (* this zeros the grade weights *)
      kid[0].letter := ' ';
      kid[0].name := filename;
      kid[0].ssn := filename;
      kid[0].comment := filename;
```

```
          for j := 1 to nograd do
            kid[0].grade[j] := -1;

          kid[0].grade[0] := 1;
          disksave;

        end;(*of create*)




   begin (* main *)




   stop := false;

   repeat


     repeat
       writeln (' enter the letter for the operation');
       writeln (' that you want :');
       writeln;
       writeln ('<c>: create a new class file');
       writeln ('<t>: enter new test scores');
       writeln ('<a>: add a new student to an existing');
       writeln ('          class');
       writeln ('<q>: quit processing');
       readln (ch1);
     until ch1 in ['c','a','t','q'];


     case ch1 of
       'c': create;
       't': begin
              diskload;
              tstadd;
              disksave;
            end;
       'a': begin
              diskload;
              repeat
                count := count + 1;
                add;
                writeln (' are there more ? (<cr> or "n")');
                readln (ch3);
              until ch3 = 'n';
              disksave;
            end;
       'q': stop := true;
     end;

   until stop = true;

   end.
```

```
program summary (input,output);

const nostud = 50;
      nograd = 20;
```

```
type student = record
               ssn,name,comment:string;
               letter:char;
               grade: array [0..nograd] of real;
             end;




var disk,outfile : file of char;
    kid: array [0..nostud] of student;
    nix,nbr,j,count,i:integer;
    range : array [0..10] of integer;



    command,filename,outname:string;






procedure newfile;
 begin
  close(outfile,lock);
  rewrite (outfile,outname);

 end;




procedure diskload;
 begin
  writeln;
  writeln ('what is the name of the class');
  writeln ('   file to be loaded?');
  readln (filename);
  reset (disk,filename);
  count:= 0;

  while not eof(disk) do
   begin


    read(disk,kid[count].letter);
    readln (disk,kid[count].ssn);
    readln (disk,kid[count].name);
    readln (disk,kid[count].comment);

    for j := 0 to nograd do
     begin
      read (disk,kid[count].grade[j]);
      if ((j > 0) and (j mod 12 = 0)) then readln (disk);
     end;

    if nograd mod 12 <> 0 then readln (disk);
    count:=count+1;
   end;

  close (disk,lock);
```

```
    count := count -1;
    writeln;
    writeln ('there are ',count,' items in the data base');
    writeln;

  end; (*of diskload*)




procedure kidave(n:integer);
 var i : integer;
     sum:real;

  begin
    sum := 0;
    kid[n].grade[0] := 0;
    for i := 1 to nograd do
     begin
       if kid[n].grade[i]>=0 then
        if kid[0].grade[i] >=  0 then
         begin
          sum := sum + kid[0].grade[i];
          kid[n].grade[0]:=kid[n].grade[0]+kid[0].grade[i]*kid[n].grade[i];
         end;
     end;

   if sum <> 0 then
     kid[n].grade[0] := kid[n].grade[0]/sum
   else kid[n].grade[0] := -1;

end;


function classave(n:integer):real;

 var i,nbr: integer;
     sum:real;
 begin

  nbr := 0;
  sum := 0;
  for i := 1 to count do
   begin
    if ((kid[i].grade[n]>=0) and (kid[i].letter = ' ')) then
     begin
      nbr := nbr + 1;
      sum := sum + kid[i].grade[n];
     end;
    end;

  writeln;
  if nbr <> 0 then classave := sum/nbr
  else classave := -1;
 end;




procedure histogram;
 var k,i,place : integer;
  begin
```

```
        newfile;
        writeln (' which test do you want ');
        writeln (' a histogram of ?');
        writeln (' (enter 0 for overall average)');
        writeln;
        readln (k);
        for place := 0 to 10 do
         range[place] := 0;

        for i := 1 to count do
         begin
          place := trunc(kid[i].grade[k]/10);
          range[place] := range[place] + 1;
         end;


        writeln (outfile);
        writeln (outfile);
        writeln (outfile,' histogram of test ',k,' scores');
        writeln (outfile);
        for i := 0 to 10 do
         begin
           for place := 0 to range[i] do
            write (outfile,'*');



          writeln (outfile,'   ',range[i],' grades in ',i*10,' to ',(i+1)*10);
         end;

   close(outfile,lock);
   end; (* of histogram *)



procedure testreport;
 begin
  newfile;
  writeln (outfile,'the overall class average is ',classave(0):5:2);
  writeln (outfile);
  writeln (outfile);

  writeln (outfile,'test#   class average   rel wt');

  writeln (outfile);
     for j := 1 to nograd do
      begin
       if kid[0].grade[j]>=0 then
        begin
         write (outfile,j,'            ',classave(j):5:1,'       ');
         writeln (outfile,kid[0].grade[j]:5:1);
        end;
      end;
   writeln (outfile);


  close (outfile,lock);
 end; (* of testreport *)



  procedure studentreport;
   begin
    newfile;
    for i := 1 to count do
     begin
      writeln (outfile);
      write (outfile,kid[i].ssn);
```

```
       write (outfile,' ',kid[i].name);
       write  (outfile,'  (*',kid[i].comment,'*)');
       writeln (outfile,'  weighted average:',kid[i].grade[0]:5:1);
       writeln (outfile);
       for j := 1 to nograd do
         if kid[0].grade[j]>=0 then
           begin
             write (outfile,'       ',j,'. ',kid[i].grade[j]:5:1);
             if (j mod  7 = 0) then writeln(outfile);
           end;
       writeln(outfile);
       writeln(outfile);
       writeln (outfile);
     end;


     writeln (outfile);

     close (outfile,lock);
  end; (* of student report *)




procedure help;
  begin
   writeln (' the following commands are valid:');
   writeln ('p--sends output to the printer');
   writeln ('c--sends output to the console');
   writeln ('h--makes histograms');
   writeln ('t--presents test summary');
   writeln ('s--present student report');
   writeln ('stop---end program');
   writeln ('help---this little message');
   writeln;
   writeln (' make a command word by combining');
   writeln (' any of these letters together');
   writeln (' for instance, the word "chpts"');
   writeln (' will send histograms to the console');
   writeln (' and send a test summary and a student');
   writeln (' summary to the printer');
   writeln;
   writeln;
  end;




begin (* main *)
 diskload;
 for i := 1 to count do kidave(i);

 outname := 'console:';
 rewrite (outfile,outname);

 writeln (outfile,'report for class ',filename);


 repeat
  writeln (' you may give a command string');
```

```
writeln ('    (type "help" for help)');
readln (command);

if command = 'help' then help else
 if command <>'stop' then
 if length(command) > 0 then
  begin
   command := concat(command,'c');
   for nix := 1 to length(command) do
    begin
     if command[nix] in ['s','p','c','h','t'] then
      begin
       case command[nix] of
        's':studentreport;
        'p': begin
              outname := 'printer:';
              newfile;
             end;
        'c': begin
              outname := 'console:';
              newfile;
             end;
        'h': histogram;
        't': testreport;

       end; (* of case *)

      end (* of then *)
     else writeln (command[nix],' not valid*****');
    end; (* of for *)

  end;

 until command = 'stop';


 close(outfile,lock);

end.
```

```
program datainq (input,output);

const nostud =  50;
      nograd = 10;


type student = record
                 ssn,name,comment:string;
                 letter:char;
                 grade: array [0..nograd] of real;
                 end;




var disk,printer  : file of char;
    kid: array [0..nostud] of student;
    nbr,j,count,i:integer;


    filename:string;

    changes,ch,ch1,ch2,ch3 : char;
```

```
procedure diskload;
 begin
  writeln;
  writeln ('what is the name of the class');
  writeln ('  file to be loaded?');
  readln (filename);
  writeln;
  writeln (' -----standby-----');
  reset (disk,filename);
  count:= 0;

  while not eof(disk) do
   begin
    read(disk,kid[count].letter);
    readln (disk,kid[count].ssn);
    readln (disk,kid[count].name);


    readln (disk,kid[count].comment);

    for j := 0 to nograd do
     begin
      read (disk,kid[count].grade[j]);
      if ((j > 0) and (j mod 12 = 0)) then readln (disk);
     end;

    if nograd mod 12 <> 0 then readln (disk);
    count:=count+1;
   end;

  close (disk,lock);

  count := count -1;
  writeln;
  writeln ('there are ',count,' items in the data base');
  writeln;

 end; (*of diskload*)




procedure disksave;
 begin
  writeln (' standby...writing to disk');
  rewrite (disk,filename);

  for i:=0 to count do
   begin
    write(disk,kid[i].letter);
    writeln (disk,kid[i].ssn);
    writeln (disk,kid[i].name);
    writeln (disk,kid[i].comment);

    for j := 0 to nograd do
     begin
      write (disk,kid[i].grade[j]:6:1);
      if ((j > 0) and (j mod 12 = 0)) then writeln(disk);
     end;

    if nograd mod 12 <> 0 then writeln (disk);
    end;
```

```
   close (disk,lock);

  end;(*of disksave*)


procedure kidave(n:integer);
 var i : integer;
     sum:real;

  begin
    sum := 0;
    kid[n].grade[0] := 0;
    for i := 1 to nograd do
     if kid[n].grade[i]>=0 then
      begin
        if kid[0].grade[i] >=  0 then
         begin
           sum := sum + kid[0].grade[i];
           kid[n].grade[0]:=kid[n].grade[0]+kid[0].grade[i]*kid[n].grade[i];
         end;
      end;
    if sum <> 0 then
     kid[n].grade[0] := kid[n].grade[0]/sum
    else kid[n].grade[0] := -1;

end;




procedure changeweights;
 var l,k : integer;
 begin
  repeat
   k := 1;
   writeln;
   writeln ('current test weights are:');
   writeln;
   writeln ('test   relative weight');
   while kid[0].grade[k]>=0 do
    begin
     writeln (k,'          ',kid[0].grade[k]:5:1);
     k := k + 1;
    end;

   writeln;
   writeln (' you may change any of these, or another');
   writeln (' but use caution if the weight you change is');
   writeln (' not mentioned here ');
   writeln;
   writeln ('change which weight ?');
   readln (l);
   writeln (' give new relative weight for test ',l);
   readln (kid[0].grade[l]);
   writeln;
   writeln (' weight ',l,' changed');
   writeln;
   writeln (' are there more changes ? (y or n)');
   readln (ch1);


  until ch1 = 'n';


  writeln ;
  writeln (' standby...all grades must be updated');
  for k := 1 to count do kidave(k);
```

```
   writeln (chr(7),'***done***');
   writeln;

end;




   procedure studentreport(i: integer);
    begin
       writeln ;
       write ( kid[i].ssn);
       write ( ' ',kid[i].name);
       write  ( '   (*',kid[i].comment,'*)');
       if kid[i].letter = 'd' then write (' *** student withdrawn ***');
       writeln ( '   weighted average:',kid[i].grade[0]:5:1);
       writeln ;
       for j := 1 to nograd do
        if kid[0].grade[j]>=0 then
         begin
          write ('       ',j,'. ',kid[i].grade[j]:5:1);
          if (j mod  6 = 0) then writeln;
         end;
       writeln;
       writeln;
       writeln ;

       writeln ;
end; (* of student report *)



   procedure printreport(i: integer);
    begin
       rewrite (printer,'printer:');
       writeln(printer) ;
       write (printer, kid[i].ssn);
       write (printer, ' ',kid[i].name);
       write  (printer, '   (*',kid[i].comment,'*)');
       if kid[i].letter = 'd' then write (printer,' *** student withdrawn ***');
       writeln (printer, '   weighted average:',kid[i].grade[0]:5:1);
       writeln(printer) ;
       for j := 1 to nograd do
        if kid[0].grade[j]>=0 then
         begin
          write (printer,'       ',j,'. ',kid[i].grade[j]:5:1);


          if (j mod  6 = 0) then writeln(printer);
         end;
       writeln(printer);
       writeln(printer);
       writeln (printer);

       writeln(printer) ;

       close(printer,lock);
end; (* of print report *)


procedure testaverage;
 var j,i,nbr : integer;
     sum : real;
 begin
  for i := 1 to count do kidave(i);
```

```
  writeln ('average which test ?');
  writeln (' (enter 0 for overall average)');
  readln (j);

  sum := 0; nbr := 0;
  for i := 1 to count do
    begin
if ((kid[i].grade[j]>=0) and (kid[0].grade[j]>=0) and (kid[i].letter=' ')) then
    begin
      nbr := nbr + 1;
      sum := sum + kid[i].grade[j];
    end;
  end;

  if nbr = 0 then writeln (' this test not recorded')
  else writeln ('average of test ',j,' is ',sum/nbr:6:1);

end; (* of testaverage *)




procedure changetestscores(var i:integer);
 var k: integer;
  begin
   writeln (' change which test score ?');
   readln (k);
   writeln (' old score on test ',k, ' is ');
   writeln (kid[i].grade[k]:6:1);
   writeln (' give new score:');
   readln (kid[i].grade[k]);
   kidave(i);
   writeln;
  end;



procedure browse;
 var i : integer;
     quit : boolean;

 begin
  i := 1;
  quit := false;

  while not quit do
   begin
    studentreport(i);

    repeat
     writeln;
     writeln ('you may :');
     writeln ('<c>: change test scores');
     writeln ('<d>: drop this student');
     writeln ('<r>: reinstate this student');
     writeln ('<p>: print report for this student');
     writeln ('<e>: escape browse');
     writeln ('<n>: go to next student');
     readln (ch2);
    until ch2 in ['p','c','d','r','e','n'];

    if ch2 <> 'n'  then
     begin
      case ch2 of
       'c': changetestscores(i);
       'd': kid[i].letter := 'd';
       'r': kid[i].letter := ' ';
       'e': quit := true;
       'p': printreport(i);
      end;
```

```
      end
    else i := i + 1;

    if i > count then quit := true;

  end; (* of while *)

end; (* of browse *)




procedure inquiry;
 var searchname : string;
     i : integer;

 begin
  writeln (' give the name or the id number for');
  writeln (' the student that you wish to inquire');
  writeln (' about ');
  readln (searchname);


  for i := 1 to count do
   begin
    if ((kid[i].name = searchname) or (kid[i].ssn = searchname))
    then
     begin
      repeat
       studentreport(i);

       repeat
        writeln (' you may:');
        writeln ('<c>: change test scores');
        writeln ('<d>: drop this student');
        writeln ('<r>: reinstate this student');
        writeln ('<q>: done with this student');
        writeln ('<p>: print report for this student');
        readln (ch3);
       until ch3 in ['p','c','d','r','q'];

       if ch3 <> 'q' then
        case ch3 of
         'c': changetestscores(i);
         'd': kid[i].letter := 'd';
         'r': kid[i].letter := ' ';
         'p': printreport(i);
        end;

      until ch3 = 'q';

     end;

   end;

  end; (* of inquiry *)




begin (* main *)
 diskload;
```

```
kid[0].letter := ' ';
for i := 1 to count do kidave(i);
repeat
 repeat
   writeln;
   writeln ('you may:');
   writeln;
   writeln ('<w>: change test weights');
   writeln ('<i>: peruse individual records');
   writeln ('<b>: browse all student records');

   writeln ('<t>: check test averages');
   writeln ('<q>: quit the program');
   writeln;
   readln (ch);

 until ch in ['w','i','b','t','q'];

 if ch <> 'q' then
   case ch of
     'w': changeweights;
     'i':inquiry;
     'b': browse;
     't': testaverage;
   end;

until ch = 'q';



writeln (' save all changes ? (y or n)');
readln (changes);
if changes <> 'n' then disksave;
end.
```

B.5   THE DATABASE SYSTEM

This system is made up of several programs. The heart of the system is the DATABASE program. See the functional diagram below:

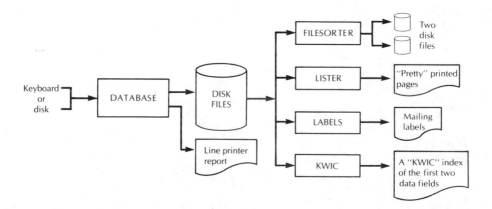

DATABASE is a general data base maintainer. It can handle many different types of data base, and its use is described on the next page.

<hr>

B.5.1   **Program DATABASE**

This program is written in a dialect of Pascal that is known as UCSD Pascal. If you have a different dialect, you will want to provide some string handling procedures, which might read and write strings. I suggest the following system:

```
type string = record
                      letter : PACKED array [1..80] of char;
                      length : 1..80;
              end;
procedure readstring (var line : string);
      begin
              line.length := 0;
              while not eoln do
                  begin
                          line.length := line.length + 1;
                          read (line.letter[line.length]);
                  end;
              readln;
      end;
procedure writestring (var line: string); var i : 1..80;
      begin
              for i := 1 to line.length do write (line.letter[i]);
              writeln;
      end;
```

If you have UCSD Pascal, you can run the program as it is. This program is a complicated one, but it has a lot of features for helping you handle data.

Suppose that you wanted to create a "little black book" of addresses. You could use this program to do so. Recall Problem 17? The program lets you add things to the little black book, delete obsolete entries, change information that becomes outdated, and search for particular entries. The result can be saved in a disk file or on the printer.

The following should provide a guide for using DATABASE.

Using DATABASE.   After you have compiled DATABASE, you are ready to run it. You will be asked whether you want a NEW or OLD data base. Since you do not yet have any data bases created, the answer is NEW.

The program asks what you want to name the data file. This will be the file that holds the output of the program, and I suggest that you use something that will remind you of the purpose of the file, such as BLACKBOOK.

DATABASE will now ask you to furnish names for each of six fields. In the program that I use, I have named the fields as follows. You may want to furnish different names for the fields.

Field 1.   NAME

Field 2.   ADDRESS

Field 3.   CITY

Field 4.   STATE

Field 5.   ZIP

Field 6.   PHONE

The program will store these names so that the next time you use BLACKBOOK it can recall them.

You are then presented with a "menu" which asks what you want to do. You can A (add to the data), S (search through the data), O (order the data into increasing order on some field), or D (save the data to disk). Be sure to do this before you E (exit the program)!

If you choose to S (search) for an entry, you will be asked a series of questions that allows you to search for almost anything. A couple of these questions may be confusing if you aren't familiar with their use.

You will be asked if you want to M (match) or N (not match) a particular field.

If you choose M, the program will give all entries that match exactly the key that you choose.

If you choose N, the program will give all entries that *do not* match the key that you choose. This is very useful for listing all entries in the data set. Just have it "not match" something absurd, such as &&&&.

By the way, if you choose PRINTER as the output file, the program will list the output on the printer.

The program can handle data files that have up to 100 entries. If you need to handle more entries, use the FILESORTER program to divide your data file into two files.

B.5.2   Auxiliary programs

Program FILESORTER.   This program takes a large data file produced by DATABASE and breaks it into two smaller data files under program control. Each of the two files may be used as input for DATABASE later on if you so desire. The reason for using FILESORTER is that the program DATABASE is limited to only 100 data items, and if it is in danger of running out of storage, FILESORTER can be used to break the large data file into two smaller ones.

Program LISTER.   This program is used to take a name and address file created by DATABASE and write a "pretty" listing on the printer. For this application, the data base fields are named, as in the example above.

Program LABELS.   This program takes the same output files from DATABASE and prints mailing labels. Even though the names in DATABASE are listed with the last name first, LABELS reverses this, so that the names are printed with the given name first and the surname second.

```
program database(input,output);

const baselimit = 100;


type
    node =   record
                  name,adr,city,state,zip,phone:string[40];
                  link:boolean;
              end;


    box = array [0..baselimit] of node;

var saveindex,start,index,count:integer;

     emptynode:node;

     list:box;

     dsk,dev:text;

     outfile,key,filename:string[40];


     cmd3set,cmd1set,cmdset: set of 'a'..'z';

     answer,select3,select1,select : char;

     gotone,match,nomatch,found,quit:boolean;



procedure readoldfile;

begin
  count:=-1;

  writeln ('what is the name of the file?');
  readln(filename);
  writeln ('standby...reading...');

  reset (dsk,filename);

  while not eof(dsk) do
    begin
     count:=count+1;
     with list[count] do
      begin
```

```
          readln (dsk,name);
          readln (dsk,adr);


          readln (dsk,city);
          readln (dsk,state);
          readln (dsk,zip);
          readln (dsk,phone);
          link:=true;
        end;

    end;

  close(dsk,lock);

  writeln;
  writeln ('*****************************');
  writeln;
  writeln ('there are ',count,' items in ',filename);
  writeln ('memory available: ',memavail);
  writeln;
  writeln ('*****************************');
  writeln;

end;(*of readoldfile*)



procedure makenewfile;

  begin
   writeln ('what will be the new file name?');
   readln (filename);

   count:=0;

   with list[count] do
    begin
     writeln (' give field definitions below:');

     writeln;
     writeln ('field one: ');
     readln (name);

     writeln;
     writeln ('field two: ');
     readln (adr);


     writeln;
     writeln ('field three: ');
     readln (city);


     writeln;
     writeln ('field four: ');
     readln (state);


     writeln;


     writeln ('field five: ');
     readln (zip);


     writeln;
     writeln ('field six: ');
     readln (phone);
```

```
        link:=true;
      end;


    rewrite (dsk,filename);

    index:=0;

    while index<=count do
     begin
      with list[index] do
       begin
        writeln (dsk,name);
        writeln (dsk,adr);
        writeln (dsk,city);
        writeln (dsk,state);
        writeln (dsk,zip);
        writeln (dsk,phone);
       end;
      index:=index+1;
     end;

  close(dsk,lock);

end; (* of makenewfile *)




procedure savefile;

  begin
   writeln ('standby...this is slow...');
   rewrite(dsk,filename);

   for index:=0 to count do
    begin
     if list[index].link = true then
     begin
       with list[index] do
        begin
         writeln (dsk,name);
         writeln (dsk,adr);
         writeln (dsk,city);
         writeln (dsk,state);
         writeln (dsk,zip);



         writeln (dsk,phone);
        end;
      end;
    end;

   close (dsk,lock);



end;(*of savefile*)




procedure menu;

  begin
   cmdset:=['a','b','c','d','e','f','g'];
```

```
         repeat begin
         with list[0] do
          begin
            writeln ('a.   ',name);
            writeln ('b.   ',adr);
            writeln ('c.   ',city);
            writeln ('d.   ',state);
            writeln ('e.   ',zip);
            writeln ('f.   ',phone);
            writeln ('g.   abort');
            writeln;
          end;

     write ('select: ');
     readln (select);

   end;

   until select in cmdset;

   end; (* of menu *)


procedure sorter;
   const m = 7;

   type str = string[40];

   var i,j,l,r : integer;
       w:node;
       tempi,tempj,x:str;
       s:0..m;
       stack: array [1..m] of
                 record l,r:integer end;


 procedure xkey(var tempx:str);
  begin

         case select of
          'a':tempx:=list[(l+r) div 2].name;

          'b':tempx := list[(l+r) div 2].adr;

          'c':tempx := list[(l+r) div 2].city;

          'd':tempx := list[(l+r) div 2].state;

          'e':tempx := list[(l+r) div 2].zip;

          'f':tempx := list[(l+r) div 2].phone;

          end; (*of case*)

     end; (* of xkey *)


 procedure ikey(var tempi:str);
  begin
          case select of
           'a':tempi := list[i].name;

           'b':tempi := list[i].adr;

           'c':tempi := list[i].city;

           'd':tempi := list[i].state;
```

```
                        'e':tempi := list[i].zip;

                        'f':tempi := list[i].phone;

                    end;(*of case*)
            end; (*of ikey*)



        procedure jkey(var tempj: str);

            begin
                case select of
                'a':tempj := list[j].name;

                'b':tempj := list[j].adr;

                'c':tempj := list[j].city;

                'd':tempj := list[j].state;

                'e':tempj := list[j].zip;

                'f':tempj := list[j].phone;

                end;(*of case*)
            end; (*of jkey*)




begin    (* main sort *)
 writeln;
 writeln ('on which field do you want to sort?');
 menu;


 if select <> 'g' then
  begin (* actual sort *)
   s := 1;
   stack[1].r := count;
   stack[1].l := 1;


   repeat
    l := stack[s].l;
    r := stack[s].r;
    s := s-1;

    repeat
     i:=l;
     j:=r;
     xkey(x);

     repeat
      ikey(tempi);
      while tempi < x do
       begin
        i:=i+1;
        ikey(tempi);
       end;

      jkey(tempj);
      while x < tempj do
       begin
```

```
        j:=j-1;
        jkey(tempj);
      end;

   if i<=j then
     begin
       w:=list[i];
       list[i]:=list[j];
       list[j]:=w;
       i:=i+1;
       j:=j-1;


     end;

   until i>j;

   if ((j-l) < (r-i)) then
     begin
       if i<r then
         begin
         s:=s+1;
         stack[s].l := i;
         stack[s].r := r;
         end;
       r:=j;
     end
   else
     begin
       if l<j then
         begin
         s:=s+1;
         stack[s].l := l;
         stack[s].r := j;
         end;
       l:=i;
     end

  until l>=r

 until s = 0;

 end;(*of if*)



end;(*of sorter*)



procedure addrecord;
 begin
  count:=count+1;
  writeln;
  write (list[0].name,':   ');
  readln (list[count].name);
  write (list[0].adr,':   ');
  readln (list[count].adr);
  write (list[0].city,':   ');
  readln (list[count].city);
  write (list[0].state,':   ');
  readln (list[count].state);
  write (list[0].zip,':   ');
  readln (list[count].zip);
  write (list[0].phone,':   ');
  readln (list[count].phone);
  writeln;
```

```
        writeln (' there are ',count,' items in the database ');
        writeln;
        list[count].link:=true;

end; (* of addrecord *)


procedure deleterecord( k:integer);

  begin
    list[k].link:=false;
  end;



procedure initial;
  begin
    emptynode.name:='empty';
    emptynode.adr:='empty';
    emptynode.city:='empty';
    emptynode.state:='empty';
    emptynode.zip:='empty';
    emptynode.phone:='empty';
    emptynode.link:=false;

    for index:=1 to baselimit do list[index]:=emptynode;

  end;

procedure changenode( k:integer);

  begin
    repeat
      begin
        quit:=false;
        writeln;
        writeln ('change which field ');
        menu;

        case select of

          'a': begin
                writeln ('old ',list[0].name,': ',list[k].name);
                write ('new: ');readln(list[k].name);
               end;


          'b': begin
                writeln ('old ',list[0].adr,': ',list[k].adr);
                write ('new: ');readln (list[k].adr);
               end;


          'c': begin

                writeln ('old ',list[0].city,': ',list[k].city);
                write  ('new: ');readln (list[k].city);
               end;


          'd': begin
                writeln ('old ',list[0].state,': ',list[k].state);
                write ('new: ');readln (list[k].state);
               end;


          'e': begin
                writeln ('old ',list[0].zip,': ',list[k].zip);
```

```
                    write ('new: ');readln (list[k].zip);
                    end;


           'f': begin
                    writeln ('old ',list[0].phone,': ',list[k].phone);
                    write ('new: ');readln(list[k].phone);
                    end;


           'g': quit:=true;

         end; (*of case*)
         end;(*of repeat*)

      until quit=true;


   end;(*of changenode*)




procedure nearmiss;

 var printit: boolean;
     index,index1:integer;

 begin
  writeln;
  writeln ('no match found...');
  writeln ('3 character match follows:');
  writeln;
  for index:=1 to count do
   begin

      with list[index] do
        begin
         printit:=true;

         for index1:=1 to 3 do


            begin
             case select of
                'a': if name[index1] <> key[index1] then printit:=false;
                'b': if adr[index1] <> key[index1] then printit:=false;
                'c': if city[index1] <> key[index1] then printit:=false;
                'd': if state[index1] <> key[index1] then printit:=false;
                'e': if zip[index1] <> key[index1] then printit:=false;
                'f': if phone[index1] <> key[index1] then printit:=false;
              end;(*case*)
            end;(*for*)


         if printit = true then
          begin
            writeln;
            writeln ('try this:');writeln;

            case select of
              'a':writeln (name);
              'b':writeln (adr);
              'c':writeln (city);
              'd':writeln (state);
              'e':writeln (zip);
              'f':writeln (phone);
```

```
                 end;(*case*)
                 writeln;
                 end; (*of then*)

           end;(*of with*)

         end;(*of outer for*)

    end;(*of procedure nearmiss*)


      procedure putit(index:integer);
       begin

           writeln(dev);
           writeln (dev,list[0].name,': ',list[index].name);
           writeln (dev,list[0].adr,': ',list[index].adr);
           writeln (dev,list[0].city,': ',list[index].city);
           writeln (dev,list[0].state,': ',list[index].state);
           writeln (dev,list[0].zip,': ',list[index].zip);
           writeln (dev,list[0].phone,': ',list[index].phone);
           writeln (dev);
           gotone:=true;
        end;(*of putit*)

   procedure search;
    begin
     quit:=false;
     gotone:=false;
     cmd1set:=['m','n'];



       repeat
         writeln;
         writeln ('do you want to ');
         writeln;
         writeln ('m.   match a key');
         writeln ('n.   complement match a key');
         readln(select);

      until select in cmd1set;

      match:=false;
      nomatch:=false;

      case select of
       'm': match:=true;
       'n': nomatch:=true;
       end;

      writeln ('key will be in what field ?');

    menu;
     if select='g' then quit:=true
      else
        begin
         writeln ('what is the key ?');
         readln (key);
         writeln;
        end;
   while quit <> true do
    begin

       writeln;

       answer:='n';
```

```
            writeln ('do you want output to an external file ?');
            readln (answer);

            outfile:='console:';

            if answer = 'y' then
             begin
              writeln;
              writeln ('what external file ?');
              readln (outfile);
             end;

              rewrite (dev,outfile);

            for index:=1 to count do
            begin
             found:=false;
             with list[index] do
              begin
                if (link = true) then


            begin
             case select of
               'a': if name=key then found:=true;
               'b': if adr=key then found:=true;
               'c': if city=key then found:=true;
               'd': if state=key then found:=true;
               'e': if zip=key then found:=true;
               'f': if phone=key then found:=true;
             end; (*of case *)

            if (((match = true) and (found = true)
            ) or ( (nomatch = true ) and not (found)))
            then
            begin
             putit(index);

             if answer  <> 'y' then
              begin

                writeln;
                writeln ('do you want to ');
                writeln ('  c.  change this record ');
                writeln ('  d.  delete this record ');
                writeln (' <cr> ignore this record ');
                readln (select1);
                 case select1 of
                   'c':changenode(index);
                   'd':deleterecord(index);
                 end; (*of case*)

             end; (*of if*)

            end; (*of if*)

          end; (*of if*)

      end; (*of with*)

    end; (*of for*)

    close (dev,lock);

    if gotone = false then nearmiss;

    quit:=true;

    end; (*of while*)

    end; (*of search*)
```

```
begin (*main program*)

 cmd3set:=['n','o'];


 initial;

 repeat
  begin
   writeln;
   writeln ('do you want to ');
   writeln ('  n.  make a new data base');
   writeln ('  o.  load an old data base');
   readln (select3);
  end;
until select3 in cmd3set;

if select3='n' then makenewfile else readoldfile;

writeln;
writeln;
cmd3set:=['a','s','d','o','e'];

repeat
 begin
  writeln;
  writeln ('do you want to ');
  writeln ('  a.  add a record');
  writeln ('  s.  search');
  writeln ('  d.  save to disk');
  writeln ('  o.  order the data');
  writeln ('  e.  end processing');

  readln (select3);

  writeln;

  case select3 of

   'a':addrecord;
   's':search;
   'd':savefile;
   'o':sorter;

  end;(* of case *)

 end;(*of repeat*)

  until select3='e';




end.
```

```
PROGRAM FILESORTER(INPUT,OUTPUT);

CONST BASELIMIT = 100;


TYPE
   NODE = RECORD
             NAME,ADR,CITY,STATE,ZIP,PHONE:STRING[40];
             LINK:BOOLEAN;
           END;
```

```
    BOX=ARRAY [0..BASELIMIT] OF NODE;


VAR INDEX,COUNT:INTEGER;

    LIST:BOX;

    DEFAULT,OTHER,DSK:TEXT;

    FILENAME,DEFAULTFILE,OTHERFILE:STRING[20];

    FLD1,FLD2,FLD3,FLD4,FLD5,FLD6:STRING;

    CH:CHAR;




PROCEDURE EXPLAIN;
 BEGIN
  WRITELN;
  WRITELN ('THIS PROGRAM IS USED TO BREAK');
  WRITELN ('A FILE INTO SEVERAL FILES');
  WRITELN;
  WRITELN ('EACH RECORD OF THE ORIGINAL FILE');
  WRITELN ('WILL BE DISPLAYED, AND YOU WILL');
  WRITELN ('BE ASKED TO SELECT ITS DESTINATION');
  WRITELN ('A <CR> WILL DEFAULT TO ONE FILE, AND');
  WRITELN ('ANY CHARACTER WILL PLACE THE RECORD');
  WRITELN ('IN THE OTHER FILE.');
  WRITELN;
 END;(*OF EXPLAIN*)



PROCEDURE READOLDFILE;


 BEGIN
  COUNT:=-1;

  WRITELN ('WHAT IS THE NAME OF THE FILE TO BE BROKEN?');
  READLN(FILENAME);

  RESET (DSK,FILENAME);

  WHILE NOT EOF(DSK) DO
   BEGIN
    COUNT:=COUNT+1;
    WITH LIST[COUNT] DO
     BEGIN
      READLN (DSK,NAME);
      READLN (DSK,ADR);
      READLN (DSK,CITY);
      READLN (DSK,STATE);
      READLN (DSK,ZIP);
      READLN (DSK,PHONE);
      LINK:=TRUE;
     END;

   END;

  CLOSE(DSK,LOCK);

  WRITELN ('THERE ARE ',COUNT,' ITEMS IN ',FILENAME);
```

```
                    WRITELN;
                    WRITELN ('MEMORY AVAILABLE IS ',MEMAVAIL);
                    WRITELN;

                    FLD1:=LIST[0].NAME;
                    FLD2:=LIST[0].ADR;
                    FLD3:=LIST[0].CITY;
                    FLD4:=LIST[0].STATE;
                    FLD5:=LIST[0].ZIP;
                    FLD6:=LIST[0].PHONE;


            END;(*OF READOLDFILE*)




            PROCEDURE SAVEOTHER;
             BEGIN
              REWRITE (OTHER,OTHERFILE);

                WRITELN (OTHER,LIST[0].NAME);
                WRITELN (OTHER,LIST[0].ADR);
                WRITELN (OTHER,LIST[0].CITY);
                WRITELN (OTHER,LIST[0].STATE);
                WRITELN (OTHER,LIST[0].ZIP);
                WRITELN (OTHER,LIST[0].PHONE);




              FOR INDEX:=1 TO COUNT DO
                BEGIN
                  IF LIST[INDEX].LINK <>TRUE THEN
                    BEGIN
                      WRITELN (OTHER,LIST[INDEX].NAME);
                      WRITELN (OTHER,LIST[INDEX].ADR);
                      WRITELN (OTHER,LIST[INDEX].CITY);
                      WRITELN (OTHER,LIST[INDEX].STATE);
                      WRITELN (OTHER,LIST[INDEX].ZIP);
                      WRITELN (OTHER,LIST[INDEX].PHONE);
                    END;(*OF IF*)
                END;(*OF FOR*)

              CLOSE (OTHER,LOCK);

            END;(*OF SAVEOTHER*)




          PROCEDURE SAVEDEFAULT;
           BEGIN
            REWRITE (DSK,DEFAULTFILE);
            FOR INDEX:=0 TO COUNT DO
              BEGIN
                IF LIST[INDEX].LINK = TRUE THEN
                  BEGIN
                    WRITELN (DSK,LIST[INDEX].NAME);
                    WRITELN (DSK,LIST[INDEX].ADR);
                    WRITELN (DSK,LIST[INDEX].CITY);
                    WRITELN (DSK,LIST[INDEX].STATE);
                    WRITELN (DSK,LIST[INDEX].ZIP);
                    WRITELN (DSK,LIST[INDEX].PHONE);

                  END;(*OF IF*)
```

```
    END; (*OF FOR*)

   CLOSE (DSK,LOCK);

  END; (*OF SAVEDEFAULT*)




BEGIN (*MAIN*)

 WRITELN;
 WRITELN;
 EXPLAIN;
 WRITELN;


 WRITELN;
 READOLDFILE;
 WRITELN;
 WRITELN;
 WRITELN ('WHAT WILL BE THE DEFAULT FILE?');
 READLN (DEFAULTFILE);
 WRITELN ('WHAT WILL BE THE NON-DEFAULT FILE ?');
 READLN (OTHERFILE);
 WRITELN;




 FOR INDEX:=1 TO COUNT DO
  BEGIN

    BEGIN
      WRITELN;
      WRITELN (FLD1,': ',LIST[INDEX].NAME);
      WRITELN (FLD2,': ',LIST[INDEX].ADR);
      WRITELN (FLD3,': ',LIST[INDEX].CITY);
      WRITELN (FLD4,': ',LIST[INDEX].STATE);
      WRITELN (FLD5,': ',LIST[INDEX].ZIP);
      WRITELN (FLD6,': ',LIST[INDEX].PHONE);
      WRITELN;

      WRITELN ('WHAT DISPOSAL FOR THIS RECORD?');
      WRITELN ('<CR> FOR ',DEFAULTFILE);
      WRITELN ('ANY CHARACTER FOR ',OTHERFILE);
      WRITELN;
      READ (CH);

      WRITELN;

      IF ORD(CH) = 32 THEN
        LIST[INDEX].LINK:=TRUE
      ELSE
        LIST[INDEX].LINK:=FALSE;


    END;

  END; (*OF FOR*)
```

```
     (*SAVEFILE SECTION*)

     SAVEDEFAULT;
     SAVEOTHER;

     END.
```

```
program labels(input,output);

const baselimit = 100;


type
  node =    record
                name,adr,city,state,zip,phone:string[40];
                link:boolean;
              end;


  box = array [0..baselimit] of node;


var n,number,nbrlabels,j,blank,index,count:integer;

      emptynode:node;

      list:box;

      dsk,dev:text;

      dummy,first,last,outfile,filename:string[40];


      select : char;




procedure readlabels(var count: integer);

 begin
  count:=0;

   while ((not eof(dsk)) and (count <= 99)) do
    begin
     count:=count+1;
     with list[count] do
      begin
        readln (dsk,name);
        readln (dsk,adr);
        readln (dsk,city);
        readln (dsk,state);
        readln (dsk,zip);
        readln (dsk,phone);
        link:=true;
      end;


    end;

  end;(* of readlabels*)
```

```
procedure initial;
 begin
  writeln ('what is the name of the file?');
  readln(filename);
 writeln ('how many labels do you want of each ');
 readln (nbrlabels);


  writeln (' what is the output file ');
  readln (outfile);
 if outfile = 'printer:' then
  begin
   writeln (' turn on printer and hit return');
   readln (select);
  end;

 rewrite (dev,outfile);
 writeln (dev); (*to dump buffer*)

  reset (dsk,filename);
  (* now read dummy first record *)

  for n := 1 to 6 do readln (dsk,dummy);


  emptynode.name:='empty';
  emptynode.adr:='empty';
  emptynode.city:='empty';
  emptynode.state:='empty';
  emptynode.zip:='empty';
  emptynode.phone:='empty';
  emptynode.link:=false;

  for index:=1 to baselimit do list[index]:=emptynode;

 end;


procedure writealabel;
 begin
   with list[index] do
    begin
     blank := pos (' ',name);
     j := length (name) - blank;
     first := copy (name,1+blank,j);
     last := copy (name,1,blank);


     for j := 1 to nbrlabels do
      begin
       writeln (dev,first,' ',last);
       writeln (dev,adr);
       writeln (dev,city,', ',state,' ',zip);
       writeln (dev);
       writeln (dev);
       writeln (dev);
      end;
     end;

end; (* of writealabel *)


procedure writelabels ( var n: integer);
 begin
  index := 1;
  while index <= n do
```

```
              begin
               writealabel;
               index := index + 1;
              end;

          end;




      begin (* main program *)

        initial;

        while not eof(dsk) do
            begin
             readlabels(n);
             writelabels (n);
            end;



        close (dsk,lock);
        close(dev,lock);


        writeln ('insert system disk and hit return ');
        readln (select);


      end.
```

```
      program lister(input,output);

      const baselimit = 100;


      type
        node =   record
                   name,adr,city,state,zip,phone:string[40];
                   link:boolean;
                 end;


        box = array [0..baselimit] of node;

      var column,place,j1,blank1,j,blank,index,count:integer;

          emptynode:node;

          list:box;

          dsk,dev:text;

          first1,last1,first,last,outfile,filename:string[40];

          buff : string;


          select : char;
```

```
procedure readoldfile;

 begin
  count:=-1;

  writeln ('what is the name of the file?');
  readln(filename);
  writeln ('standby...reading...');

  reset (dsk,filename);

  while not eof(dsk) do
   begin
    count:=count+1;
    with list[count] do
     begin
       readln (dsk,name);
       readln (dsk,adr);
       readln (dsk,city);

       readln (dsk,state);
       readln (dsk,zip);
       readln (dsk,phone);
       link:=true;
      end;

   end;

  close(dsk,lock);

  writeln;
  writeln ('*****************************');
  writeln;
  writeln ('there are ',count,' items in ',filename);
  writeln ('memory available: ',memavail);
  writeln;
  writeln ('*****************************');
  writeln;

 end;(*of readoldfile*)




procedure initial;
 begin
  emptynode.name:='empty';
  emptynode.adr:='empty';
  emptynode.city:='empty';
  emptynode.state:='empty';
  emptynode.zip:='empty';
  emptynode.phone:='empty';
  emptynode.link:=false;

  for index:=1 to baselimit do list[index]:=emptynode;

 end;



procedure lastone;
 begin
   writeln (dev,list[count].name);
   writeln (dev,list[count].adr);
 writeln (dev,list[count].city,', ',list[count].state,' ',list[count].zip);
   writeln (dev,list[count].phone);
   writeln (dev);
   writeln (dev);
```

```
    end;


begin (* main program *)


  initial;
  readoldfile;


  writeln (' what is the output file ');
  readln (outfile);
  if outfile = 'printer:' then
   begin
    writeln (' turn on printer and hit return');
    readln (select);
   end;


  place := (count div 2)*2;


  rewrite (dev,outfile);
  writeln (dev); (* to clear buffer*)
  writeln (dev);

  for index := 1 to 40 - (length(filename) div 2) do
   write (dev,' ');

  writeln (dev,filename);
  writeln (dev);
  writeln (dev);
  writeln (dev);


  index := 1;

  while index < place do
    begin

      write (dev,list[index].name);
      column := length (list[index].name);
      while column <= 39 do
       begin
        write (dev,' ');
        column := column + 1;
       end;

      writeln (dev,list[1+index].name);
      write (dev,list[index].adr);
      column := length (list[index].adr);
      while column <= 39 do
       begin
        write (dev,' ');
        column := column + 1;
       end;

      writeln (dev,list[1+index].adr);
buff := concat(list[index].city,', ',list[index].state,' ',list[index].zip);

write (dev,buff);


column := length(buff);
    while column <= 39 do
      begin
        write (dev,' ');
```

```
        column := column + 1;
      end;

 buff :=concat(list[1 + index].city,', ',list[1 + index].state);
 buff := concat (buff,' ',list[1 + index].zip);
    writeln (dev,buff);

    write (dev,list[index].phone);
    column := length (list[index].phone);
    while column <=39 do
     begin
       write (dev,' ');
       column := column + 1;
     end;

    writeln (dev,list[1+index].phone);
    writeln (dev);
    writeln (dev);
    index := index + 2;
   end;

 if ( place  <> count) then
  lastone;


 close (dev,lock);



 end.
```

Program FORMLETTER.   This program uses data files that are created by DATABASE to place name-and-address information on form letters. One feature of the program is that it can vary the salutation of the letter according to your tastes.

The actual letter that you send is created by using the system editor to create a text file which contains the main body of the letter, including the closing.

FORMLETTER expects that the addresses are in a DATABASE file with the fields specified as follows:

Field 1.   LASTNAME FIRSTNAME

Field 2.   STREET ADDRESS

Field 3.   CITY

Field 4.   STATE

Field 5.   ZIP

Field 6.   PHONE

The program contains directions for its own use.

```
        program formletter(input,output);

        type entry = record
                       name,adr,city,state,
                       zip, phone : string[40];
                     end;


        var line : array [1..66] of string[80];

            person : array [1..10] of entry;

            x,y,i,n,n1 : integer;

            letterfile,infile,outfile : file of char;

            lettername,inname,outname : string[30];

            ch : char;

            first,last,salute : string;


            done : boolean;



        procedure readpeople;
         begin
          n := 1;

          done := false;

          while ((n <= 10) and (not eof(infile))) do
           begin

            if not eof(infile) then
             with person[n] do
              begin
                readln (infile,name);
                readln (infile,adr );
                readln (infile,city);
                readln (infile,state);
                readln (infile,zip);
                readln (infile,phone);
                n := n + 1;
              end;

           end; (* of while *)

             n := n - 1;

            if eof (infile) then
             begin
               done := true;


             end;

         end; (* of readpeople *)




        procedure readletter;
         begin
```

```
writeln (' what is the letter file ?');
readln (lettername);
reset (letterfile,lettername);

n1 := 0;

while not eof(letterfile) do
 begin
  n1 := n1 + 1;
  if not eof(letterfile) then
   readln (letterfile,line[n1]);
  end;

n1 := n1 -1;

close(letterfile,lock);
end; (* of readletter *)




procedure init1;
 begin
  writeln (' what is the addressfile ?');
  readln (inname);
  writeln (' what is the output file ?');
  readln (outname);
  writeln (' be sure that ',outname,' is available ');
  writeln ('  and hit return ');
  readln (ch);

(* now open all files *)

 reset (infile,inname);
 rewrite (outfile,outname);

 (* get first dummy record from dbms file *)

 with person[1] do
  begin
   readln (infile,name);
   readln (infile,adr);
   readln (infile,city);
   readln (infile,state);
   readln (infile, zip);




   readln (infile, phone);
  end;


end; (* of init1 *)

procedure init2;
 begin
  (* now invent salutation *)

  writeln;
  writeln ('your letter can have a personalized');
  writeln (' salutation.');
  writeln (' we will now build it.  please input');
  writeln (' a string that tells how you want ');
  writeln (' the salutation to appear.  this');
  writeln (' string will include a "1" whereever');
  writeln (' you want the first name, and a "2"');
  writeln (' wherever you want the last name.');
  writeln (' for example, the string');
```

```
            writeln (' "dear 1 2:"');
            writeln (' will cause the computer to write ');
            writeln (' (for instance)');
            writeln (' "dear bill walker:"');

            writeln;
            writeln (' giving the string "dear 1," will');
            writeln (' cause the salutation to appear as ');
            writeln (' "dear bill,"');
            writeln;
            writeln (' the string "2-" would cause ');
            writeln (' the salutation "walker-" to appear.');
            writeln;
            writeln (' now enter the salutation string');
            readln (salute);



            (* here we will invent the proper headings *)


        end; (* of initialize *)




    procedure putsalute;
     var j: integer;

     begin
      j := 1;
      while j <= length(salute) do


        begin
         if ((salute[j] = '1') or (salute[j] = '2'))
         then
          case salute[j] of
           '1': write (outfile,first);
           '2': write (outfile,last);
          end
         else write (outfile,salute[j]);

         j := j + 1;
        end; (* of while *)

      writeln (outfile);
     end; (* of putsalute *)



    procedure putheading(var person : entry);
     begin
      x := pos(' ',person.name);
      y := length(person.name) - x;
      first := copy (person.name,x+1,y);
      last := copy (person.name,1,x);

     (* now we will put the heading *)
     writeln (outfile,first,' ',last);
     writeln (outfile,person.adr);
     writeln (outfile,person.city,', ',person.state,' ',person.zip);
     writeln (outfile);

     end; (* of putheading *)
```

```
procedure putletter;
 var i : integer;
 begin
  for i := 1 to n1 do
    writeln (outfile,line[i]);
  end;




begin (* sample main *);

 init1;
 init2;
 readletter;


 writeln (' *****letter read ****');


 writeln;
 repeat
  readpeople;
  i := 1;
  while i <= n do
   begin
     page (outfile);
     putheading(person[i]);
     putsalute;
     putletter;
     i := i + 1;
   end;
 until done = true;

 close (infile,lock);
 close (outfile, lock);
 close (letterfile,lock);

 end.
```

B.5.3   The KWIC index

A Key Word In Context (KWIC) index is a special computer-generated listing of titles of articles. Using a KWIC index, it is easy to identify the magazine articles that are of interest to you in some particular context. This can be a great help when you must do research in your personal library.

KWIC works like this: Suppose that you are given the title of an article. That title includes several important words, called *key words*. There may also be several unimportant words in the title, such as *and, the,* or *a.*

The KWIC index lists all the key words of article titles alphabetically, so that it is easy to find the name of the article you are looking for.

For instance, suppose an article is entitled "Ghost Dance among the

Sioux." We have arbitrarily decided that key words are those words that have four or more letters; so this article would be listed under *Ghost, Dance, among,* and *Sioux,* but not under *the.* If we look in the KWIC index under *Ghost,* we find "Ghost Dance among the Sioux/// . . . AICC March 1972," which indicates that this article appeared in *American Indian Crafts and Culture* for March 1972. We could look under *Sioux* and find "Sioux///Ghost Dance among the . . . AICC March 1972," which is a description of the same article, only listed differently.

The article "Hopi Snake Dance" would appear in the index under *Hopi* or *Snake* or *Dance.* Any of these listings would tell us that the article appeared in *Whispering Wind* for December 1977.

Programs KWIC and MERGETREES are designed to help you create a KWIC index of a data file created by DATABASE. For this application, we suggest that DATABASE be used to create a data base that has its fields defined as follows:

Field 1. TITLE AND AUTHOR

Field 2. LOCATION OF ARTICLE

Field 3. Unused

Field 4. Unused

Field 5. Unused

The KWIC index will be made by varying the words which are entered into Field 1. Field 2 will be printed, but the other fields will not.

Output will consist of some variation of Field 1, followed by an exact listing of Field 2, and no other fields.

In this fashion, you index your library by authors and by variations on the titles but not by location of the book—although the location of each book will be printed.

In the process of making a KWIC index, the program creates several (up to 10) temporary files. If you desire more than one copy of the KWIC index, use the program MERGETREES to merge these files into one large KWIC index. This saves quite a bit of processing time compared to running KWIC several times. The temporary files may be removed after you are done.

MERGETREES actually is a 10-way merge sort and can be used as such.

```
PROGRAM KWIC (INPUT,OUTPUT);

TYPE PTR = ^ NODE;
     NODE = RECORD
              TITLE:STRING;
              DATE: STRING;
              LEFT,RIGHT: PTR;
            END;
```

```
VAR    LISTING: ARRAY [1..10] OF NODE;
       FILENBR,INDEX,NBRLISTINGS,I,J,K: INTEGER;
       HEAD,P,Q,R: PTR;
       VOLUME,INFILE,NEWTITLE,FILENAME: STRING;
       OUTFILE,DEV: TEXT;
       NAMES:ARRAY [1..10] OF STRING;
       HEAP1,HEAP:^INTEGER;


PROCEDURE INITIAL;
 VAR I: INTEGER;
     CH: CHAR;

 BEGIN
  WRITELN (' WHAT IS THE SCRATCH VOLUME ');
  READLN (VOLUME);
  WRITELN (' BE SURE ',VOLUME, ' IS AVAILABLE AND HIT RETURN ');
  READLN (CH);
  NAMES[1] := 'F1.TMP';
  NAMES[2] := 'F2.TMP';
  NAMES[3] := 'F3.TMP';
  NAMES[4] := 'F4.TMP';
  NAMES[5] := 'F5.TMP';
  NAMES[6] := 'F6.TMP';
  NAMES[7] := 'F7.TMP';
  NAMES[8] := 'F8.TMP';
  NAMES[9] := 'F9.TMP';
  NAMES[10] := 'F10.TMP';

  FOR I := 1 TO 10 DO
   NAMES[I] := CONCAT(VOLUME,NAMES[I]);

 END;


PROCEDURE ADD(P:PTR);
 BEGIN
  IF NEWTITLE <= P^.TITLE THEN
   IF P^.LEFT = NIL THEN P^.LEFT := Q
   ELSE ADD(P^.LEFT)

  ELSE
   IF P^.RIGHT = NIL THEN P^.RIGHT := Q
   ELSE ADD(P^.RIGHT);
 END;


PROCEDURE LIST(P:PTR);
 BEGIN
  IF P <> NIL THEN
   BEGIN
    LIST(P^.LEFT);
    WRITELN (OUTFILE,P^.TITLE,'...',P^.DATE);
    LIST(P^.RIGHT);
   END;
  END;
```

```
PROCEDURE GITNODE (VAR Q:PTR);
 BEGIN
  NEW(Q);
 END;




PROCEDURE LOADTITLES;
 BEGIN
  I := 0;
  WHILE ( (I < 10) AND (NOT EOF(DEV))) DO
   BEGIN
    I := I + 1;
    READLN (DEV,LISTING[I].TITLE);

    READLN (DEV,LISTING[I].DATE);
    READLN (DEV);
    READLN (DEV);
    READLN (DEV);
    READLN (DEV);
   END;

   NBRLISTINGS := I;
 END;




PROCEDURE MAKETREE (VAR HEAD:PTR; VAR TITLE:STRING);
 VAR ENDOFTITLE, STOP: BOOLEAN;
     OLDPLACE,PLACE: INTEGER;

 BEGIN
  IF LENGTH (TITLE) > 0 THEN ENDOFTITLE := FALSE
  ELSE ENDOFTITLE := TRUE;

  PLACE := 1;
  OLDPLACE := 1;


  WHILE NOT ENDOFTITLE DO
   BEGIN
    STOP := FALSE;

   REPEAT
    IF PLACE = LENGTH(TITLE) THEN
     BEGIN
      STOP := TRUE;
      ENDOFTITLE := TRUE;
     END;
    IF TITLE[PLACE] = ' ' THEN STOP := TRUE;
    PLACE := PLACE + 1;
   UNTIL STOP = TRUE;


   IF ((PLACE - OLDPLACE > 4) )THEN
       BEGIN
         NEWTITLE := CONCAT(COPY(TITLE,OLDPLACE,1 + LENGTH(TITLE)-OLDPLACE),
          '//',COPY (TITLE,1,OLDPLACE-1));

         GITNODE(Q);
         Q^.TITLE := NEWTITLE;
```

```
                            Q^.LEFT := NIL;
                            Q^.RIGHT := NIL;
                            Q^.DATE := LISTING[INDEX].DATE;
                            IF HEAD =NIL THEN HEAD := Q
                            ELSE ADD(HEAD);




                  END;
             OLDPLACE := PLACE;

       END;


       END;




PROCEDURE MERGETREES;

TYPE LISTPTR = ^LISTNODE;
     LISTNODE = RECORD
                   TITLE:STRING;
                   LINK:LISTPTR;
                END;




VAR LAST1,FRONT1 : ARRAY [1..10] OF LISTPTR;

    F1,F2,F3,F4,F5,F6,F7,F8,F9,F10 : TEXT;

    AVAIL1,Q1 : LISTPTR;

    OUTDEV1 : TEXT;

    LINECOUNT1,TOTAL1, SMALL,I1,NBRF1 : INTEGER;

    INF1,OUT1,TEST1 : STRING;

    CH1: CHAR;

    STOP1, DONE1 : BOOLEAN;




PROCEDURE PRINT (VAR LINE : STRING);
 BEGIN
  LINECOUNT1 := LINECOUNT1 + 1;

  IF LINECOUNT1 > 60 THEN
   BEGIN
     WRITELN (OUTDEV1);
     WRITELN (OUTDEV1);
     WRITELN (OUTDEV1);
     WRITELN (OUTDEV1);
     WRITELN (OUTDEV1);
     WRITELN (OUTDEV1);


   LINECOUNT1 := 1;
  END;
```

```
        WRITELN (OUTDEV1,LINE);
      END;




   FUNCTION ENDOF (VAR I1: INTEGER):BOOLEAN;
    BEGIN
     CASE I1 OF
      1: ENDOF := EOF(F1);
      2: ENDOF := EOF(F2);
      3: ENDOF := EOF(F3);
      4: ENDOF := EOF(F4);
      5: ENDOF := EOF(F5);
      6: ENDOF := EOF(F6);
      7: ENDOF := EOF(F7);
      8: ENDOF := EOF(F8);
      9: ENDOF := EOF(F9);
      10: ENDOF := EOF(F10);
     END;
    END;




   PROCEDURE KILL (VAR Q1: LISTPTR);
    BEGIN
     Q1^.LINK := AVAIL1;
     AVAIL1 := Q1;
    END;


   PROCEDURE GIT (VAR Q1: LISTPTR);
    BEGIN
     IF AVAIL1 = NIL THEN NEW(Q1)
     ELSE
      BEGIN
       Q1 := AVAIL1;
       AVAIL1 := AVAIL1^.LINK;
      END;
    END;




   PROCEDURE INITIAL;
    BEGIN
     NBRF1 := FILENBR;
     WRITELN (' OUTPUT TO WHAT FILE ?');
     READLN (OUT1);
     WRITELN (' BE SURE ',OUT1,' IS AVAILABLE AND HIT RETURN');
     READLN (CH1);
     AVAIL1 := NIL;



     FOR I1 := 1 TO NBRF1 DO
      BEGIN
       FRONT1[I1] := NIL;
       LAST1[I1] := NIL;
      END;

     TOTAL1 := 0;

     WRITELN (' STANDBY...TAKES TIME...');
     REWRITE (OUTDEV1,OUT1);

     LINECOUNT1 := 0;

    END;
```

```
PROCEDURE LOADBUFFER(VAR I1: INTEGER);
 VAR COUNT : INTEGER;

 BEGIN
  COUNT := 0;

  WHILE ((NOT ENDOF(I1)) AND (COUNT < 10)) DO
   BEGIN
    GIT(Q1);
    DONE1 := FALSE;
    CASE I1 OF
     1: READLN (F1,Q1^.TITLE);
     2: READLN (F2,Q1^.TITLE);
     3: READLN (F3,Q1^.TITLE);
     4: READLN (F4,Q1^.TITLE);
     5: READLN (F5,Q1^.TITLE);
     6: READLN (F6,Q1^.TITLE);
     7: READLN (F7,Q1^.TITLE);
     8: READLN (F8,Q1^.TITLE);
     9: READLN (F9,Q1^.TITLE);
     10: READLN (F10,Q1^.TITLE);
    END;

    Q1^.LINK := NIL;

    IF FRONT1[I1] = NIL THEN
     FRONT1[I1] := Q1
    ELSE
     LAST1[I1]^.LINK := Q1;

    LAST1[I1] := Q1;

    COUNT := COUNT + 1;
   END;

 END;


PROCEDURE MERGE;
 BEGIN
  FOR I1 := 1 TO NBRF1 DO
   IF FRONT1[I1] = NIL THEN
     LOADBUFFER(I1);

   BEGIN
    SMALL := 0;
    TEST1 := 'ZZZZZZZZZZZZZZZZZZZZZZZZ';

    FOR I1 := 1 TO NBRF1 DO
     BEGIN
      IF FRONT1[I1] <> NIL THEN
       IF FRONT1[I1]^.TITLE < TEST1 THEN
        BEGIN
         TEST1 := FRONT1[I1]^.TITLE;
         SMALL := I1;
        END;
     END;

    IF SMALL = 0 THEN DONE1 := TRUE
    ELSE
     BEGIN
      PRINT (TEST1);
      TOTAL1 := TOTAL1 + 1;
      Q1 := FRONT1[SMALL];
      FRONT1[SMALL] := FRONT1[SMALL]^.LINK;
      KILL(Q1);
     END;

   END;

 END;
```

```
PROCEDURE CLOSEIT(VAR I1:INTEGER);
 BEGIN
  CASE I1 OF
   1: CLOSE(F1,LOCK);
   2: CLOSE(F2,LOCK);
   3: CLOSE(F3,LOCK);
   4: CLOSE(F4,LOCK);
   5: CLOSE(F5,LOCK);
   6: CLOSE(F6,LOCK);
   7: CLOSE(F7,LOCK);
   8: CLOSE(F8,LOCK);
   9: CLOSE(F9,LOCK);
   10: CLOSE(F10,LOCK);
  END;



END;


PROCEDURE OPENIT (VAR I1: INTEGER);
 BEGIN
  CASE I1 OF
   1: RESET (F1,NAMES[1]);
   2: RESET (F2,NAMES[2]);
   3: RESET (F3,NAMES[3]);
   4: RESET (F4,NAMES[4]);
   5: RESET (F5,NAMES[5]);
   6: RESET (F6,NAMES[6]);
   7: RESET (F7,NAMES[7]);
   8: RESET (F8,NAMES[8]);
   9: RESET (F9,NAMES[9]);
   10: RESET (F10,NAMES[10]);
  END;
END;




BEGIN (* MAIN OF PROCEDURE MERGETREES *)

 INITIAL;
 FOR I1 := 1 TO NBRF1 DO OPENIT(I1);


   DONE1 := TRUE;

   FOR I1 := 1 TO NBRF1 DO
    IF ENDOF(I1) = FALSE THEN
      IF FRONT1[I1] = NIL THEN LOADBUFFER(I1);

   IF NOT DONE1 THEN
    BEGIN
     REPEAT
      MERGE;
     UNTIL DONE1 = TRUE;
    END;

 WRITELN ('TOTAL ENTRIES WRITTEN : ',TOTAL1);

 FOR I1 := 1 TO NBRF1 DO CLOSEIT(I1);

 CLOSE (OUTDEV1,LOCK);
 WRITELN (' PUT IN BOOT DISKETTE AND HIT RETURN');
 READLN (CH1);

END;
```

```
BEGIN (* MAIN *)
 INITIAL;
 HEAD := NIL;
 WRITELN (' WHAT IS THE DATA FILE ?');
 READLN (INFILE);
 WRITELN (' STANDBY...TAKES A WHILE ');
 RESET (DEV,INFILE);

 READLN (DEV);
 READLN (DEV);
 READLN (DEV);
 READLN (DEV);
 READLN (DEV);
 READLN (DEV);

 FILENBR := 1;
 MARK (HEAP1);
 REPEAT
  BEGIN
   FILENAME := NAMES[FILENBR];
   WRITELN (' MAKING TEMPORARY FILE  ',FILENAME);
   LOADTITLES;

   MARK(HEAP);
   FOR INDEX := 1 TO NBRLISTINGS DO
    MAKETREE(HEAD,LISTING[INDEX].TITLE);

   WRITELN ('TREE ',FILENAME,' BEING WRITTEN');
   WRITELN;
   REWRITE (OUTFILE,FILENAME);
   LIST(HEAD) ;
   CLOSE (OUTFILE,LOCK);
   RELEASE (HEAP);
   HEAD:= NIL;
   FILENBR := FILENBR + 1;
  END
 UNTIL EOF(DEV);

 CLOSE (DEV,LOCK);
 FILENBR := FILENBR -1;
 RELEASE (HEAP1);
 MERGETREES;
END.
```

```
PROGRAM MERGETREES (INPUT,OUTPUT);

TYPE PTR = ^NODE;
     NODE = RECORD
              TITLE:STRING;
              LINK:PTR;
            END;



VAR LAST,FRONT : ARRAY [1..10] OF PTR;

    F1,F2,F3,F4,F5,F6,F7,F8,F9,F10 : TEXT;

    AVAIL,Q : PTR;

    OUTDEV : TEXT;

    LINECOUNT,TOTAL, SMALL,I,NBRFILES : INTEGER;

    INFILE,OUTFILE,TEST : STRING;
```

```
            CH: CHAR;

            STOP, DONE : BOOLEAN;

            NAMES : ARRAY [1..10] OF STRING;



PROCEDURE PRINT (VAR LINE : STRING);
 BEGIN
  LINECOUNT := LINECOUNT + 1;

   IF LINECOUNT > 60 THEN
    BEGIN
     WRITELN (OUTDEV);
     WRITELN (OUTDEV);
     WRITELN (OUTDEV);
     WRITELN (OUTDEV);
     WRITELN (OUTDEV);
     WRITELN (OUTDEV);
     LINECOUNT := 1;
    END;

   WRITELN (OUTDEV,LINE);
 END;




FUNCTION ENDOF (VAR I: INTEGER):BOOLEAN;



 BEGIN
  CASE I OF
    1: ENDOF := EOF(F1);
    2: ENDOF := EOF(F2);
    3: ENDOF := EOF(F3);
    4: ENDOF := EOF(F4);
    5: ENDOF := EOF(F5);
    6: ENDOF := EOF(F6);
    7: ENDOF := EOF(F7);
    8: ENDOF := EOF(F8);
    9: ENDOF := EOF(F9);
    10: ENDOF :- EOF(F10);
  END;
 END;



PROCEDURE KILL (VAR Q: PTR);
 BEGIN
  Q^.LINK := AVAIL;
  AVAIL := Q;
 END;


PROCEDURE GIT (VAR Q: PTR);
 BEGIN
  IF AVAIL = NIL THEN NEW(Q)
   ELSE
    BEGIN
     Q := AVAIL;
     AVAIL := AVAIL^.LINK;
    END;
 END;
```

```
PROCEDURE INITIAL;
 BEGIN
  WRITELN ('HOW MANY FILES ARE TO BE MERGED ?');
  READLN (NBRFILES);
  WRITELN (' INPUT FROM WHAT VOLUME ?');
  READLN (INFILE);
  WRITELN (' BE SURE ',INFILE,' IS AVAILABLE AND HIT RETURN');
  READLN (CH);
  WRITELN (' OUTPUT TO WHAT FILE ?');
  READLN (OUTFILE);
  WRITELN (' BE SURE ',OUTFILE,' IS AVAILABLE AND HIT RETURN');
  READLN (CH);
  AVAIL := NIL;
  FOR I := 1 TO NBRFILES DO
   BEGIN
    FRONT[I] := NIL;
    LAST[I] := NIL;
   END;


  TOTAL := 0;
  NAMES[1] := CONCAT(INFILE,'F1.TMP');
  NAMES[2] := CONCAT (INFILE,'F2.TMP');
  NAMES[3] := CONCAT (INFILE,'F3.TMP');
  NAMES[4] := CONCAT (INFILE,'F4.TMP');
  NAMES[5] := CONCAT (INFILE,'F5.TMP');
  NAMES[6] := CONCAT (INFILE,'F6.TMP');
  NAMES[7] := CONCAT (INFILE,'F7.TMP');
  NAMES[8] := CONCAT (INFILE,'F8.TMP');
  NAMES[9] := CONCAT (INFILE,'F9.TMP');
  NAMES[10] := CONCAT(INFILE,'F10.TMP');

  REWRITE (OUTDEV,OUTFILE);

  LINECOUNT := 0;

 END;




PROCEDURE LOADBUFFER(VAR I: INTEGER);
 VAR COUNT : INTEGER;

 BEGIN
  COUNT := 0;

  WHILE ((NOT ENDOF(I)) AND (COUNT < 10)) DO
   BEGIN
    GIT(Q);
    DONE := FALSE;
    CASE I OF
     1: READLN (F1,Q^.TITLE);
     2: READLN (F2,Q^.TITLE);
     3: READLN (F3,Q^.TITLE);
     4: READLN (F4,Q^.TITLE);
     5: READLN (F5,Q^.TITLE);
     6: READLN (F6,Q^.TITLE);
     7: READLN (F7,Q^.TITLE);
     8: READLN (F8,Q^.TITLE);
     9: READLN (F9,Q^.TITLE);
     10: READLN (F10,Q^.TITLE);
    END;

    Q^.LINK := NIL;

    IF FRONT[I] = NIL THEN
     FRONT[I] := Q
```

```
        ELSE
          LAST[I]^.LINK := Q;

        LAST[I] := Q;

        COUNT := COUNT + 1;
      END;


    END;



PROCEDURE MERGE;
  BEGIN
    FOR I := 1 TO NBRFILES DO
      IF FRONT[I] = NIL THEN
        LOADBUFFER(I);


      BEGIN
        SMALL := O;
        TEST := 'ZZZZZZZZZZZZZZZZZZZZZZZZZ';

        FOR I := 1 TO NBRFILES DO
          BEGIN
            IF FRONT[I] <> NIL THEN
              IF FRONT[I]^.TITLE < TEST THEN
                BEGIN
                  TEST := FRONT[I]^.TITLE;
                  SMALL := I;
                END;
          END;

        IF SMALL = 0 THEN DONE := TRUE
        ELSE
          BEGIN
            PRINT (TEST);
            TOTAL := TOTAL + 1;
            Q := FRONT[SMALL];
            FRONT[SMALL] := FRONT[SMALL]^.LINK;
            KILL(Q);
          END;

      END;

  END;



PROCEDURE CLOSEIT(VAR I:INTEGER);
  BEGIN
    CASE I OF
      1: CLOSE(F1,LOCK);
      2: CLOSE(F2,LOCK);
      3: CLOSE(F3,LOCK);
      4: CLOSE(F4,LOCK);
      5: CLOSE(F5,LOCK);
      6: CLOSE(F6,LOCK);
      7: CLOSE(F7,LOCK);
      8: CLOSE(F8,LOCK);
      9: CLOSE(F9,LOCK);
      10: CLOSE(F10,LOCK);
    END;
  END;
```

```
PROCEDURE OPENIT (VAR I: INTEGER);
 BEGIN
  CASE I OF
   1: RESET  (F1,NAMES[1]);
   2: RESET  (F2,NAMES[2]);
   3: RESET  (F3,NAMES[3]);
   4: RESET  (F4,NAMES[4]);
   5: RESET  (F5,NAMES[5]);
   6: RESET  (F6,NAMES[6]);
   7: RESET  (F7,NAMES[7]);
   8: RESET  (F8,NAMES[8]);
   9: RESET  (F9,NAMES[9]);
   10: RESET  (F10,NAMES[10]);
  END;
 END;




BEGIN (* MAIN *)

 INITIAL;
 FOR I := 1 TO NBRFILES DO OPENIT(I);


   DONE := TRUE;

   FOR I := 1 TO NBRFILES DO
    IF ENDOF(I) = FALSE THEN
      IF FRONT[I] = NIL THEN LOADBUFFER(I);

   IF NOT DONE THEN
    BEGIN
     REPEAT
      MERGE;
     UNTIL DONE = TRUE;
    END;

 WRITELN ('TOTAL ENTRIES WRITTEN : ',TOTAL);

 FOR I := 1 TO NBRFILES DO CLOSEIT(I);

 CLOSE (OUTDEV,LOCK);
 WRITELN (' PUT IN APPLE0: AND HIT RETURN');
 READLN (CH);

END.
```

Index*

*Includes section and page numbers.

*This book has been set Linotron 202,
In 10 and 9 point Optima, leaded 2 points.
Chapter numbers and titles are 20 point
Optima. The size of the type page is
31 by 48 picas.*

Date Due